Macmillan
Mathematics
Pupil's book

2B

Paul Broadbent & Mary Ruddle

MACMILLAN

Contents

BLOCK D   Addition and subtraction to 999

BLOCK E   Geometry

BLOCK F Measures and data

Odd and even numbers

Odd numbers always end in: 1   3   5   7   9

Even numbers always end in: 0   2   4   6   8

13	21	16	20
★★★★★★ ★★★★★★ ★	★★★★★★★★★★ ★★★★★★★★★★ ★	★★★★★★★★ ★★★★★★★★	★★★★★★★★★★ ★★★★★★★★★★

Even numbers can be put into 2 equal groups.
Odd numbers always have 1 left over.

1   Write odd or even for each number.
Look at the units digit to help.

a) 24	**b)** 15	**c)** 30	**d)** 29
e) 17	**f)** 42	**g)** 21	**h)** 16

2   Draw jumps above the lines to show odd numbers.
Draw jumps below the lines to show even numbers.

a)

b)

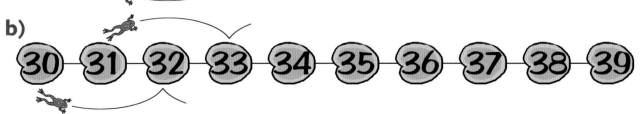

3 Sort these numbers into 2 groups. Write a list of all the odd numbers and all the even numbers.

Odd	Even

25

28

32

50

49

6

23

54

31   47

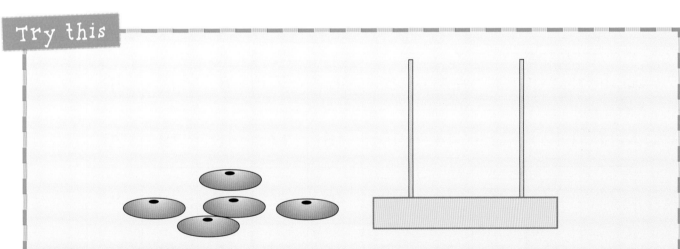

Try this

Draw an abacus.
Draw 5 beads on the abacus and write the number you have made.
Is the number odd or even?

Make a list of the odd numbers you can make on an abacus using 5 beads.

Make a list of the even numbers you can make on an abacus using 5 beads.

Patterns on grids

Look for patterns in number grids.

Count in 2s to find the red numbers.
Count in 5s to find the bold numbers.

1	2	3	4	**5**
6	7	8	9	**10**
11	12	13	14	**15**
16	17	18	19	**20**
21	22	23	24	**25**

1 Continue the patterns on this grid.

1	2	3	4	5	6	7	8	9	10
11	12	13	14	15	16	17	18	19	20
21	22	23	24	25	26	27	28	29	30
31	32	33	34	35	36	37	38	39	40

a) Count in 2s and shade each number.

b) Count in 4s and circle each number.

c) Count in 5s and cross each number.

2 Draw these patterns on a 100 square.

- Colour blue → the numbers 5, 10, 15 and continue colouring each number as you count in 5s.

- Cross X → 10, 20, 30 and continue crossing the numbers as you count in 10s.

What do you notice about these patterns?

1	2	3	4	5	6	7	8	9	10
11	12	13	14	15	16	17	18	19	20
21	22	23	24	25	26	27	28	29	30
31	32	33	34	35	36	37	38	39	40
41	42	43	44	45	46	47	48	49	50
51	52	53	54	55	56	57	58	59	60
61	62	63	64	65	66	67	68	69	70
71	72	73	74	75	76	77	78	79	80
81	82	83	84	85	86	87	88	89	90
91	92	93	94	95	96	97	98	99	100

Try this

Complete this 100-square.

Count in 2s, 3s, 4s, 5s and 10s and look at the patterns on the grid.

	99			95					
									90
							73		
			64	65	66	67			
		43							50
40									31
21				25					
20			17	16				12	11
1	2	3							10

Number patterns

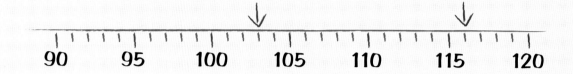

Look at the numbers on this number line. You can count in steps of 5.

90   95   100   105   110   115   120

Which numbers are the arrows pointing to?

103 and 116

1 Write the missing numbers on each number line.

a)

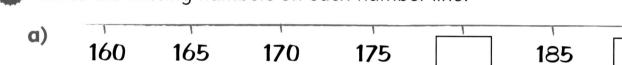

160   165   170   175   [ ]   185   [ ]

b)

132   134   136   [ ]   [ ]   142   144

c)

60   70   [ ]   90   100   [ ]   120

d)

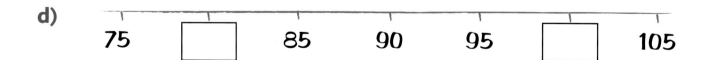

75   [ ]   85   90   95   [ ]   105

e)

240   250   [ ]   [ ]   280   290   300

f)

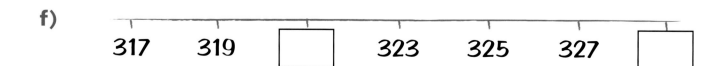

317   319   [ ]   323   325   327   [ ]

2 Write the next two numbers in each sequence.

a)

100	110	120		

b)

454	456	458		

c)

560	570	580		

d)

125	130	135		

e)

193	195	197		

f)

370	375	380		

3 Write the next three numbers in each sequence.

a)

160	170	180			

b)

195	197	199			

c)

234	236	238			

d)

410	420	430			

e)

345	350	355			

f)

620	622	624			

Try this

Count back in steps and write the next two numbers.

a) 138   136   134   132   ☐   ☐

b) 140   130   120   110   ☐   ☐

c) 200   195   190   185   ☐   ☐

Comparing numbers to 999

Which is the greater number, 258 or 285?

When you need to compare numbers, look carefully at the **digits**.

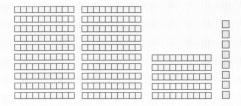 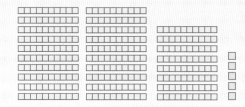

- 258 is 200 + 50 + 8
- 285 is 200 + 80 + 5

- Compare the hundreds, then the tens and then the units.
- 80 is greater than 50, so 285 is greater than 258.

1 Write the smaller number in each pair.

a)
231 213

b) 196 149

c) 317 462

d) 628 188

e)
273 236

f) 437 435

g) 624 642

h) 263 265

i) 518 427

j)
270 291

k)
646 636

l) 284 289

2 Write the greatest number in each set.

a) 291   295   259   b) 138   118   148

c) 255   162   226   d) 413   431   416

e) 227   224   229   f) 784   679   780

g) 326   363   332   h) 527   570   572

3 Colour the largest number in each pair.

 a)  135   153   b)  180   160

c) 172   144   d) 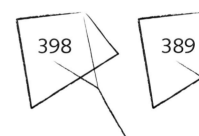 398   389

e)  214   240   f) 635   572

g) 759   806

Ordering numbers to 999

To put 3-digit numbers in order, look at the **hundreds** digit first.
If any of the hundreds are the same then compare the **tens** digits.
If any tens are the same then compare the **units** digits.

These numbers are in order, starting with the smallest.

Smallest: 427
              429
              538
Greatest: 584

1 Write these numbers in order. Start with the smallest.

a) 471 413 326 383

b) 293 198 289 273

c) 358 361 316 368

d) 529 575 625 679

e) 414 448 484 418

f) 255 165 756 151

2 Join these numbers in order. Start with the smallest.

a)

 236   262   263

229   226

b)

414   449

419   494   499

c)

278   277   385

355   357

d)

533

644

531   534   643

Assessment

Put these numbers in order, starting with the smallest.
What are the next five numbers in each sequence?

a) 143   139   141   137   145   147

b) 650   635   645   630   640   655

c) 480   510   530   490   500   520

Rounding to the nearest 10

Rounding numbers to the nearest 10 makes them easier to work with.

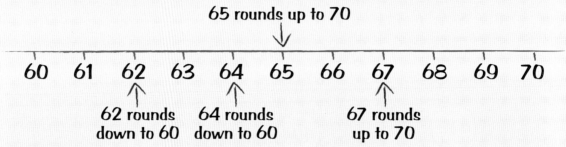

65 rounds up to 70

60 61 62 63 64 65 66 67 68 69 70

62 rounds   64 rounds   67 rounds
down to 60   down to 60   up to 70

Round down if the units digit is less than 5.
Round up if the units digit is 5 or more.

When numbers are rounded we get an approximate answer.

Example

49 + 37 is approximately 50 + 40 = 90
The answer to 49 + 37 is 86, so 90 is a good estimate.

1 Circle the number that is the nearest 10 for each of these.

a) 34   30   40

b) 76   70   80

c) 45   40   50

d) 58   50   60

e) 87   80   90

f) 25   20   30

g) 74   70   80

h) 66   60   70

2 Round these numbers to the nearest 10.

a) 36 → ☐   b) 85 → ☐

c) 42 → ☐   d) 18 → ☐

e) 79 → ☐   f) 29 → ☐

g) 72 → ☐   h) 85 → ☐

3 Round each number to the nearest 10 to find an approximate answer.

Example
23 + 12 is approximately 20 + 10 = 30

a) 19 + 23 is approximately ☐

b) 25 + 37 is approximately ☐

c) 38 + 45 is approximately ☐

d) 46 + 32 is approximately ☐

e) 86 – 39 is approximately ☐

f) 59 – 23 is approximately ☐

g) 81 – 28 is approximately ☐

h) 57 – 26 is approximately ☐

Adding 2-digit numbers: short method

When you add numbers, always work out an approximate answer in your head.

Example

34 + 48   Approximate answer: 30 + 50 = 80

Step 1 Add the units

```
    T  U
   ¹3  4
 + 4  8
 _____
    2
```

4 add 8 is 12. Write the 2 units and write 1 ten in the tens column.

Step 2 Add the tens

```
    T  U
   ¹3  4
 + 4  8
 _____
   8  2
```

Add together 3 tens, 4 tens and 1 ten and write 8 tens.

---

1 Answer these.

a)
```
   3 8
 + 2 3
 _____
```

b)
```
   4 8
 + 2 4
 _____
```

c)
```
   4 3
 + 3 8
 _____
```

d)
```
   2 6
 + 4 7
 _____
```

e)
```
   5 9
 + 2 9
 _____
```

f)
```
   1 6
 + 6 8
 _____
```

2 Add these. Use the space to work them out.

a) 44 + 48 = ☐

b) 22 + 39 = ☐

c) 67 + 14 = ☐

d) 35 + 37 = ☐

e) 13 + 28 = ☐

f) 69 + 29 = ☐

g) 36 + 47 = ☐

h) 17 + 38 = ☐

i) 39 + 54 = ☐

j) 25 + 26 = ☐

Try this

Choose pairs of numbers from the grid which total 52.
Write five addition sums.

25	43	36	38
14	16	9	45
19	7	33	27

☐ + ☐ = 52

☐ + ☐ = 52

☐ + ☐ = 52

☐ + ☐ = 52

☐ + ☐ = 52

Adding and subtracting hundreds

Use a number line from 0 to 900 to help you add and subtract hundreds.

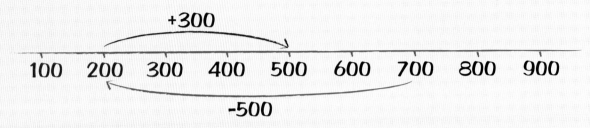

$$200 + 300 = 500 \qquad 700 - 500 = 200$$

1 Answer these.

a) 200 + 500 = ☐

b) 100 + 400 = ☐

c) 600 + 300 = ☐

d) 400 + 400 = ☐

e) 700 + 100 = ☐

f) 300 + 500 = ☐

g) 600 – 200 = ☐

h) 500 – 100 = ☐

i) 900 – 700 = ☐

j) 700 – 300 = ☐

k) 800 – 500 = ☐

l) 900 – 400 = ☐

2 Write the missing numbers in each chain.

a)

700 − 200 = ◯ − 100 = ◯ + 400 = ◯

b)

200 + 500 = ◯ − 300 = ◯ + 200 = ◯

c)

800 − 300 = ◯ + 400 = ◯ − 700 = ◯

d)

500 + 200 = ◯ − 100 = ◯ − 500 = ◯

3 The three outside numbers total the centre number.
Write the missing numbers.

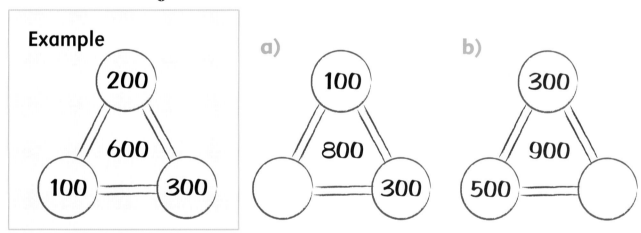

Example

200
600
100 = 300

a)

100
800
◯ = 300

b)

300
900
500 = ◯

Try this

Find different ways to complete this.

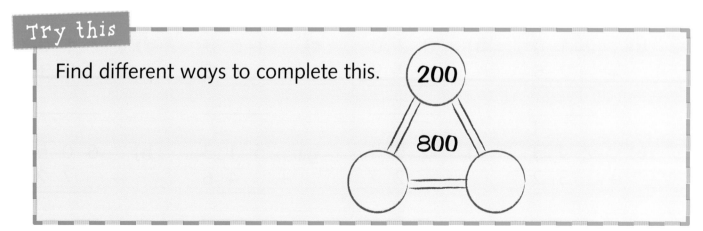

200
800
◯ ◯

Adding 3-digit numbers: no exchange

To add 3-digit numbers, break them up into hundreds, tens and units.

Add together 213 and 345

Hundreds	Tens	Units
2	1	3
3	4	5
5	5	8

$$200 + 10 + 3$$
$$+ \ 300 + 40 + 5$$
$$\overline{500 + 50 + 8}$$

$$
\begin{array}{r}
2\ 1\ 3 \\
+\ 3\ 4\ 5 \\
\hline
5\ 5\ 8
\end{array}
$$

Add the units, then the tens and then the hundreds.

1 Answer these.

a)
$$
\begin{array}{r}
2\ 1\ 0 \\
+\ \ \ \ 2\ 5 \\
\hline
\end{array}
$$

b)
$$
\begin{array}{r}
3\ 2\ 0 \\
+\ \ \ \ 2\ 9 \\
\hline
\end{array}
$$

c)
$$
\begin{array}{r}
4\ 5\ 0 \\
+\ \ \ \ 3\ 6 \\
\hline
\end{array}
$$

d)
$$
\begin{array}{r}
7\ 1\ 0 \\
+\ \ \ \ 5\ 3 \\
\hline
\end{array}
$$

e)
$$
\begin{array}{r}
2\ 4\ 3 \\
+\ \ \ \ 3\ 2 \\
\hline
\end{array}
$$

f)
$$
\begin{array}{r}
2\ 5\ 1 \\
+\ \ \ \ 2\ 7 \\
\hline
\end{array}
$$

g)
$$
\begin{array}{r}
5\ 1\ 3 \\
+\ \ \ \ 4\ 6 \\
\hline
\end{array}
$$

h)
$$
\begin{array}{r}
6\ 0\ 5 \\
+\ \ \ \ 7\ 2 \\
\hline
\end{array}
$$

2 Answer these.

a)   2 3 6
    + 4 2 1
    _____

b)   4 2 4
    + 4 2 5
    _____

c)   3 0 6
    + 6 7 2
    _____

d)   5 4 0
    + 1 1 5
    _____

e)   2 5 3
    + 2 1 4
    _____

f)   3 4 2
    + 5 4 7
    _____

g)   1 6 6
    + 2 0 2
    _____

h)   2 2 3
    + 4 1 2
    _____

3 Find the total for each addition. Draw a line to match each bee to the correct sum. Make up an addition for the extra answer.

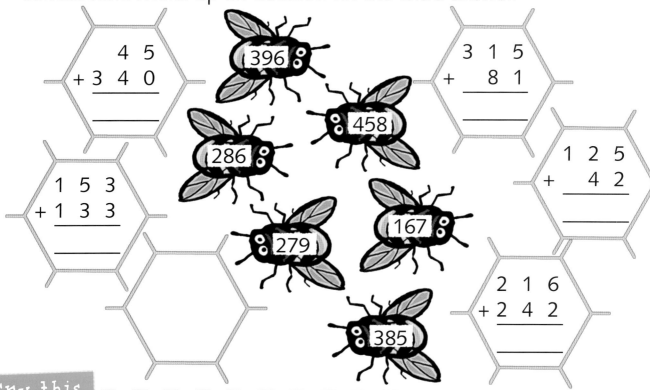

     4 5
   + 3 4 0
   _____

    396

    3 1 5
   +   8 1
   _____

    458

    286

   1 5 3
   + 1 3 3
   _____

    1 2 5
   +   4 2
   _____

    167

    279

    2 1 6
   + 2 4 2
   _____

    385

Write the missing digits in these.

a)
     4 ☐ 8
   + 5 2 ☐
   _____
   ☐   4 8

b)
   ☐ 3 ☐
   + 1 ☐ 3
   _____
   2 7 6

c)
     6 ☐ 4
   + ☐ 5 1
   _____
   8 7 ☐

Subtracting 3-digit numbers: no exchange

To subtract 3-digit numbers, break them up into hundreds, tens and units.

What is 357 take away 124?

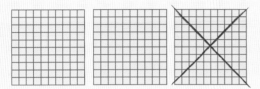 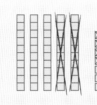

$$300 + 50 + 7$$
$$- 100 + 20 + 4$$
$$\overline{200 + 30 + 3}$$

$$\begin{array}{r} 3\ 5\ 7 \\ -\ 1\ 2\ 4 \\ \hline 2\ 3\ 3 \end{array}$$

Subtract the units, then the tens and then the hundreds.

1 Answer these.

a)
```
  3 5 6
-   2 0
-------
```

b)
```
  4 9 2
-   5 0
-------
```

c)
```
  2 4 5
-   3 1
-------
```

d)
```
  7 8 7
-   6 3
-------
```

e)
```
  9 8 2
-   4 1
-------
```

f)
```
  6 3 8
-   1 7
-------
```

g)
```
  4 7 8
-   5 3
-------
```

h)
```
  8 3 9
-   2 8
-------
```

2 Answer these.

a)
```
   3 8 5
 - 1 2 0
 -------
```

b)
```
   6 3 8
 - 4 2 0
 -------
```

c)
```
   5 7 7
 - 2 3 1
 -------
```

d)
```
   6 9 4
 - 2 5 3
 -------
```

e)
```
   5 3 2
 - 2 0 1
 -------
```

f)
```
   4 0 9
 - 3 0 2
 -------
```

g)
```
   9 5 1
 - 3 5 0
 -------
```

h)
```
   6 1 9
 - 2 1 7
 -------
```

Assessment

Write the missing digits in these. The first one has been done for you.

a)
```
   [2] 4   6
 +  5  [4] 3
 -----------
    7  8  [9]
```

b)
```
   [ ]  9  [ ]
 +  1  [ ]  3
 -----------
    6   9   7
```

c)
```
   [ ] [ ]  9
 -  1  5   1
 ----------
    6  3  [ ]
```

d)
```
    9  [ ]  6
 -  [ ]  4  1
 -----------
    5   3  [ ]
```

Coins and notes

These are some of the coins and notes we use.

Cents can be written as ¢   Dollars can be written as $
10 cents ➜ 10¢   5 dollars ➜ $5

Look at the differences between these coins and notes.

1¢   5¢   10¢   25¢ $1 $5

100¢ = $1

1 What can you buy for these exact amounts?

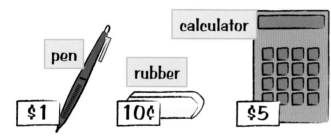

pen $1   rubber 10¢   calculator $5

 pencil 25¢

 chalk 50¢

a)

b)

c)

d)

e)

2 Which is worth most? Complete each sentence.

a)

[ ] is worth more than [ ]

b)

[ ] is worth more than [ ]

c)

[ ] is worth more than [ ]

d)

[ ] is worth more than [ ]

3 Join these coins and notes in order, starting with the highest value.

Equivalence

50 cents can be made in different ways.
Can you find other ways to make 50¢?

1 Find pairs with the same value. Write the value and the two matching letters.

a)
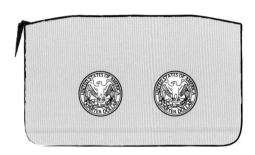

b)

c)
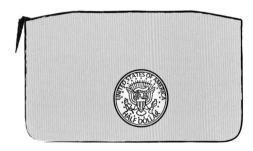

d)

e)

f)

2 Complete these tables.

a) Number of 5¢ coins

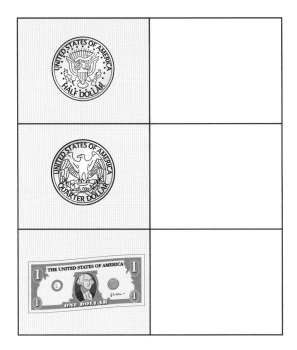

b) Number of 25¢ coins

3 Draw coins in each purse.

a) Draw 2 coins to make $1

b) Draw 4 coins to make $1

c) Draw 10 coins to make $1

d) Draw 3 coins to make $1

Try this

I have three coins in my pocket.
All the coins have the same value.
The total is less than $1 and more than 50¢.
How much money have I got in my pocket?

Making totals

25¢ + 10¢ + 10¢ + 10¢ + 5¢ = 60¢

1 Draw any three coins to match each price.

a) 16¢

b) 51¢

c) 60¢

d) 27¢

e) 30¢

f) 55¢

2 Total each amount.

a) Max has 30¢ and Sophie has 35¢. Together they have

b) Laura has 55¢ and Lily has 25¢. Together they have

c) Emma has 40¢ and Charlie has 35¢. Together they have

3 Total these.

a) 35¢ + 45¢ =   **b)** 60¢ + 15¢ =   **c)** 40¢ + 30¢ =

d) 20¢ + 25¢ =   **e)** 50¢ + 15¢ =   **f)** 30¢ + 65¢ =

g)   1 5¢   **h)**   3 0¢   **i)**   2 5¢   **j)**   2 5¢
    + 5 5¢   + 6 0¢   + 3 5¢   + 6 5¢
    ———   ———   ———   ———

Try this

What different totals can you make with any three of these coins?

Giving change

Example

A pump costs 85¢. What is the change from $1?

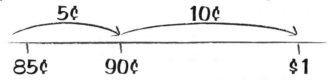

5¢	10¢
85¢ → 90¢	→ $1

Count on from 85¢ to 90¢ and then on to $1. The change is 15¢.

1 Use the number line to count on. Write the change from $1.

a) 75¢ → change from $1 = ☐

5¢   20¢
75¢   80¢ $1

b) 35¢ → change from $1 = ☐

5¢   60¢
35¢   40¢ $1

c) 45¢ → change from $1 = ☐

5¢   50¢
45¢   50¢ $1

d) 65¢ → change from $1 = ☐

5¢   30¢
65¢   70¢ $1

e) 55¢ → change from $1 = ☐

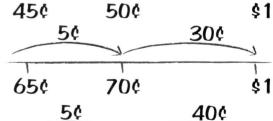

5¢   40¢
55¢   60¢ $1

f) 25¢ → change from $1 = ☐

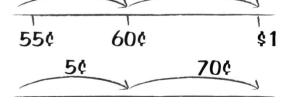

5¢   70¢
25¢   30¢ $1

2 $1 is used to buy these items. Write the change.

a) 95¢ → $1 → Change: [ ] ¢

b)  80¢ → $1 → Change: [ ] ¢

c)  65¢ → $1 → Change: [ ] ¢

d)  55¢ → $1 → Change: [ ] ¢

e) 70¢ → $1 → Change: [ ] ¢

f)  85¢ → $1 → Change: [ ] ¢

g) 60¢ → $1 → Change: [ ] ¢

h)  45¢ → $1 → Change: [ ] ¢

Try this

I buy a cake from a bakery. I am given three identical coins as change from $1. What could be the possible cost of the cake?

Money problems

Use these four steps to solve word problems.

1 Read the problem.
2 Sort out the calculation.
3 Work out the answer.
4 Check back.

Example

A board game costs $17.
It is reduced in price by $9.
What is the new price?

$17 − $9 = $8

The new price of the game is $8.
Check: $8 + $9 = $17

1 Read and answer these.

a) A t-shirt costs $4. How much would four t-shirts cost?

b)  What is the total price of a kite at $20 and a toy train at $17?

c)  A coat normally costs $58, but it is reduced by $20. How much does the coat cost now?

d)  Harry has saved $65 and William has saved $32. How much more does Harry have than William?

e)  How much would it cost to buy three pens at $7 each?

f)  How much change would you get from $50 if you bought a belt for $33?

g)  Lily pays a taxi $19 to go to the hospital and $17 to go from the hospital into town.
How much does she spend on taxi fares in total?

h)  Two plants cost $73 together. One plant is $42, so how much is the other plant?

2 Each vase has been bought with $20. Join the correct change to each price.

> Your change is eight dollars. Here is a five dollar note and three one dollar notes.

> Eleven dollars, thank you. Here is your nine dollars change.

> Here is your change. It is three dollars.

> Thank you. Your change will be a five dollar note and a one dollar note.

> I have two dollars change to give back. Thank you.

 $12

 $17

 $11

 $14

 $18

Assessment

1 A ball costs $7. Alex pays the exact amount with three notes. Which notes does he use?

2 Two coins were given as change when Megan paid for a drink with a $1 note. If the drink cost 65¢, which two coins were given as change?

3 A football shirt costs $28 and the shorts cost $16. How much is this in total?

Numbers and number patterns

1 Write the missing numbers in these sequences.

a)

| 45 | 47 | 49 | | | 55 | |

b)

| 96 | | | | 104 | 106 | 108 |

c)

| 230 | 240 | | 260 | 270 | | |

d)

| 350 | 355 | | | 370 | 375 | |

e)

| 410 | 412 | | | 418 | | 422 |

f)

| 297 | 299 | | 303 | 305 | | |

2 Complete this 100-square.

Count in 2s, 3s, 4s, 5s and 10s and look at the patterns on the grid.

1	2	3						9	10
			14						20
21				25					
			34	35	36				
		53							60
61						67			70
71									
								89	
		94							

3 Look at these price labels.
Compare them and write the highest price.

a) $79 $74   b) $102 $111   c) $192 $197

d) $141 $139   e) $203 $199   f) $311 $309

4 Look at these numbers.

a) Which is the smallest number?

b) Which is the largest number?

c) Which numbers are greater than 500?

d) Write the numbers in order, starting with the smallest.

Try this

Use the digits 3, 4 and 5.

Make as many different 1-digit, 2-digit and 3-digit numbers as you can.
Write them in order, starting with the smallest.

Addition and subtraction to 999

1 These are adding machines. What numbers will come out of each machine?

Write an approximate answer first and then work out the answer.

a)

28

39

15

26

37

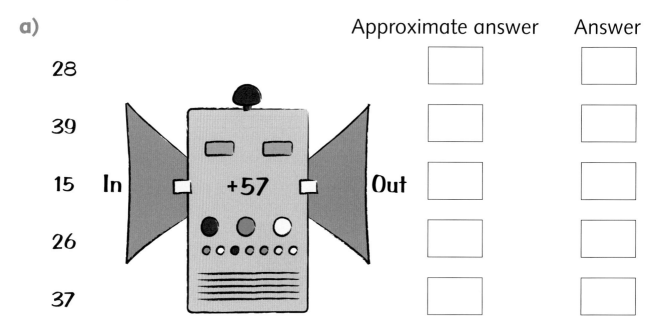

Approximate answer	Answer

b)

55

27

49

38

46

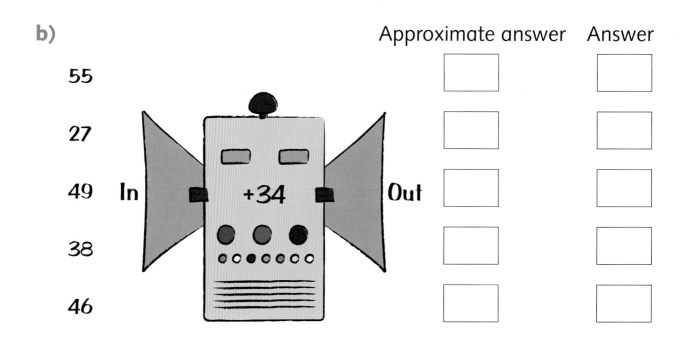

Approximate answer	Answer

2 Complete these addition walls.

a)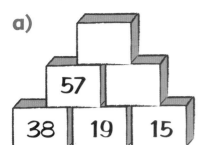

57

| 38 | 19 | 15 |

b)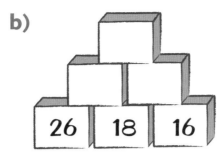

| 26 | 18 | 16 |

c)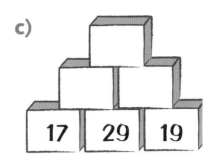

| 17 | 29 | 19 |

3 Answer these.

a)
```
  1 5 2
+ 7 2 0
───────
```

b)
```
  6 3 1
+ 2 4 7
───────
```

c)
```
  1 4 6
+ 3 4 3
───────
```

d)
```
  8 3 5
- 4 2 0
───────
```

e)
```
  5 1 8
- 3 0 7
───────
```

f)
```
  9 4 6
- 1 3 4
───────
```

4 Complete these.

a)
```
  □ 3 6
+ 5 2 □
───────
  7 □ 6
```

b)
```
  □ 3 □
+ 4 □ 7
───────
  5 4 9
```

c)
```
  3 4 5
+ □ 4 □
───────
  6 □ 9
```

d)
```
  9 3 □
- □ 2 1
───────
  6 □ 7
```

e)
```
  8 5 □
- 1 □ 3
───────
  □ 1 6
```

f)
```
  7 □ 6
- □ 5 2
───────
  5 3 □
```

Try this

Find five different ways to complete each of these.

□ + □ = 750   □ − □ = 250

Money

1 Draw coins that you could use to pay for these.

a)  30¢
b)  85¢
c)  56¢
d) 27¢

2 Write these coins and notes in order, starting with the smallest.

a)

b)

c) Which coins could you use to make $1?

3 Write the change from 50 cents for each of these.

a) 35¢ → Change = ☐

b) 25¢ → Change = ☐

c) 40¢ → Change = ☐

d) 20¢ → Change = ☐

e) 15¢ → Change = ☐

f) 45¢ → Change = ☐

g) 5¢ → Change = ☐

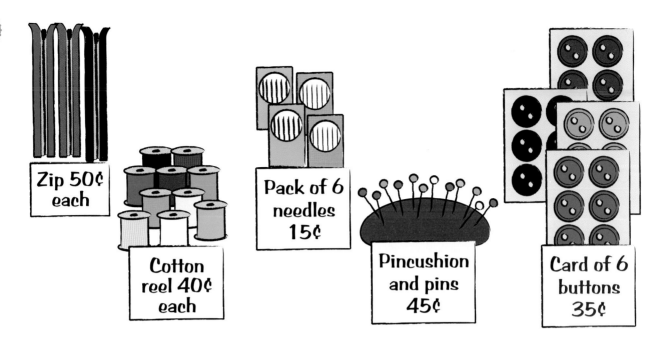

Write the total cost for each of these.

a)   b)   c)

d)   e)   f)

5 Each shopping bill is paid with $50. Tick the bills which will get exactly $5 in change.

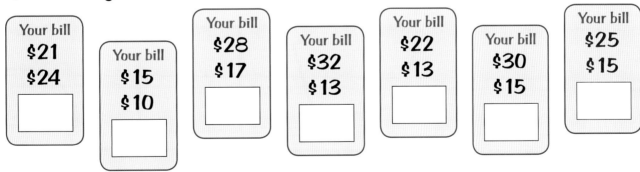

Your bill
$21
$24

Your bill
$15
$10

Your bill
$28
$17

Your bill
$32
$13

Your bill
$22
$13

Your bill
$30
$15

Your bill
$25
$15

Assessment

What change from $100 would you get for each of the totals above?

Open and closed shapes

Compare these shapes.

Open shape   Closed shape

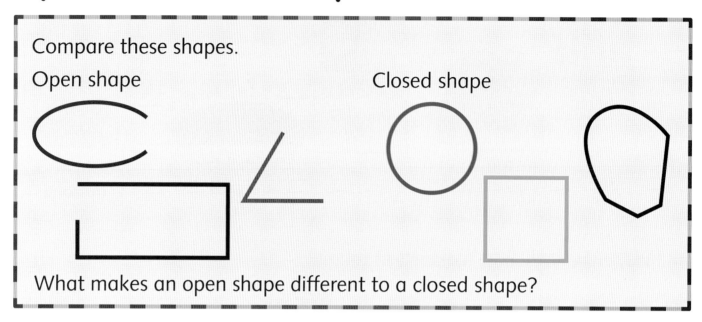

What makes an open shape different to a closed shape?

1 Look at these shapes. Sort them into open and closed shapes.
Write the letters in the correct part of the chart.

Open	Closed

A

B

C

D

E

F

G

H

I

J

K

L

2 These are all open shapes. Draw one more straight line on each shape to make them closed shapes.

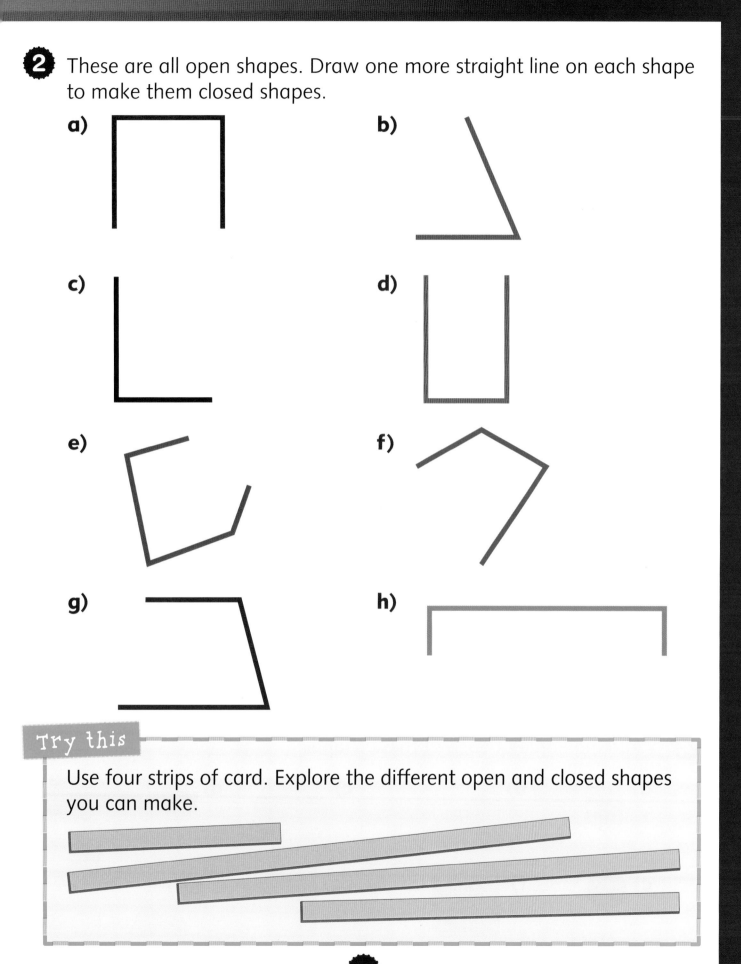

a)

b)

c)

d)

e)

f)

g)

h)

Try this

Use four strips of card. Explore the different open and closed shapes you can make.

41

Comparing flat shapes

These are the names of some closed shapes.

square   rectangle   triangle   circle

How are these flat shapes similar?
How are they different?

1 Complete this chart. Write the shape letters in the correct sections.

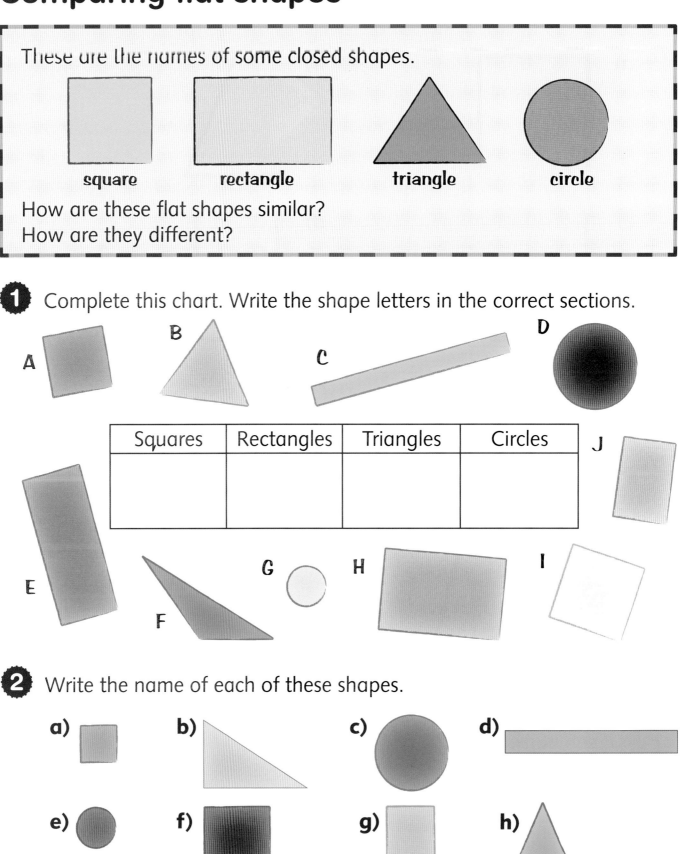

Squares	Rectangles	Triangles	Circles

2 Write the name of each of these shapes.

a)   b)   c)   d)

e)   f)   g)   h)

42

3 Colour the shapes in this picture. Use the colours given in the chart.

Colour	Shape
red	circles
blue	rectangles
yellow	triangles
green	squares

Comparing solid shapes

Solid shapes are all around us. Learn the names of these solid shapes.

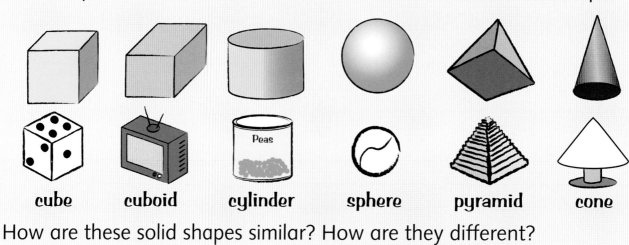

cube   cuboid   cylinder   sphere   pyramid   cone

How are these solid shapes similar? How are they different?

1 Write the name of the odd shape out in each set.

a)

b)

c)

d)

e)

f)

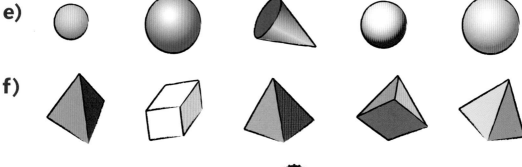

2 Write the name of each shape.

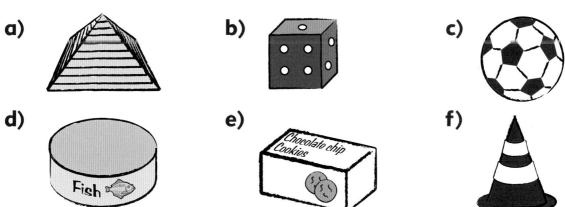

a)

b)

c)

d)

Fish

e) Chocolate chip Cookies

f)

3 Match each shape to its name.

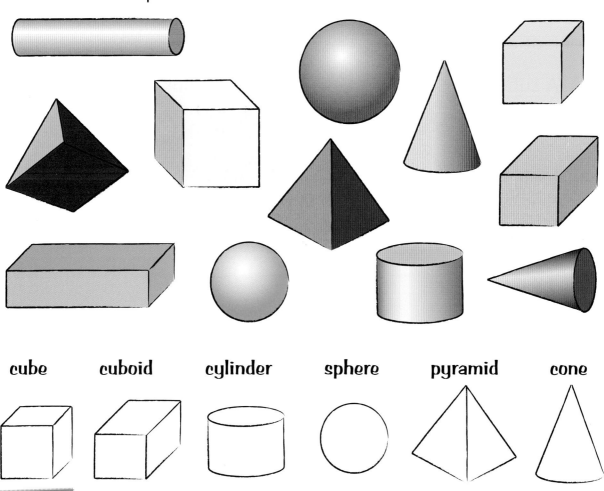

cube   cuboid   cylinder   sphere   pyramid   cone

Try this

Look for shapes of objects around you.
Draw the objects and write the names of the shapes.

Cubes and cuboids

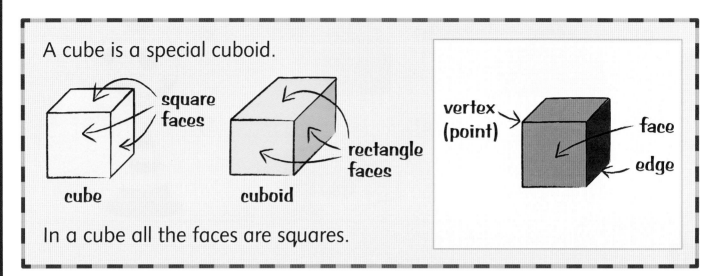

A cube is a special cuboid.

square faces

cube

rectangle faces

cuboid

vertex (point)

face

edge

In a cube all the faces are squares.

1 Look at a model of a cube. Complete these.

a) A cube has ☐ faces.   **b)** A cube has ☐ edges.

c) A cube has ☐ vertices.   **d)** Is this the same for a cuboid?

2 For each of these objects write **cube**, **cuboid**, or **not a cuboid or cube**.

a) dice

_____

b) ball

_____

c) house brick

_____

d) tin

_____

e) toy brick

_____

f)  box

_____

3 Look at these cuboids.

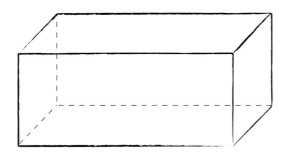 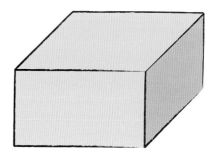

Complete these.

a) A cuboid has ☐ faces.

b) A cuboid has ☐ edges.

c) A cuboid has ☐ vertices (corners).

4 Answer these.

a) I am a shape with 6 faces, all my edges are exactly the same length. What shape am I?

b) I am a shape with 12 edges and 6 rectangle faces. What shape am I?

c) I am a shape with 8 vertices and all faces exactly the same size and shape. What shape am I?

d) I am a shape with 4 long edges all the same length and 8 short edges all the same length. What shape am I?

Properties of solid shapes

When you are comparing solid shapes, look at their properties: faces, edges and vertices.

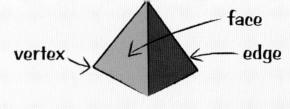

A cylinder has a curved face and 2 flat faces.

A cube has 6 square faces.

1 Look at these shapes. Write the correct shape letters to answers these.

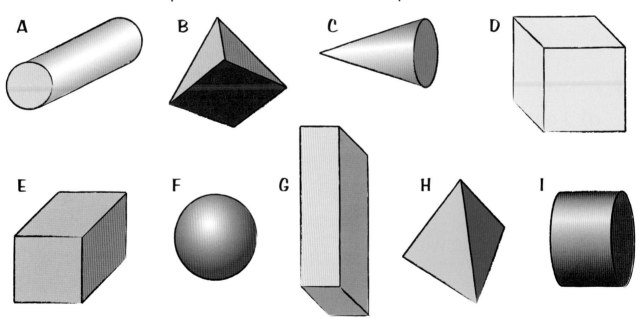

a) Which shapes have curved faces?
b) Which shapes have one or more square face?
c) Which shape has no edges?
d) Which shapes have no vertices?
e) Which shapes have more than 10 edges?
f) Which shape has 5 vertices?

2 Write the missing number of faces and vertices for each of these shapes.

a)

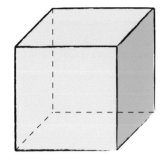

☐ square faces

8 vertices

b)

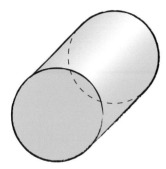

☐ circle faces

1 curved face

0 vertices

c)

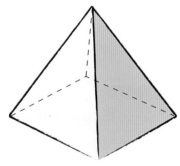

1 square face

☐ triangle faces

☐ vertices

Name and describe these solid shapes.
What are the shapes of the blue faces?

a) 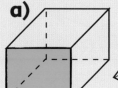   b) 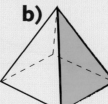   c) 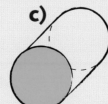   d) 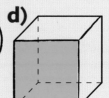   e) 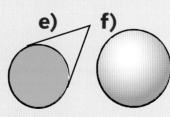   f)

Lines, segments and rays

A **line** is a group of points on a straight path. It goes on and on for ever. This line is called line AB.

A **line segment** is a part of a line that has two end points. This line segment is called segment CD.

A **ray** is part of a line. It has one end point and the other end goes on and on for ever. A ray is named with its end point first followed by any other point on the ray.

This ray is called ray EF.

1 Write whether these are examples of lines, segments or rays.

Example

ray XY

a)

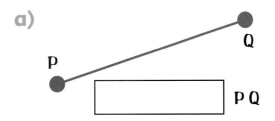

P Q

b)

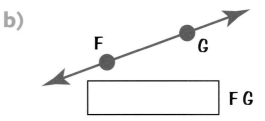

F G

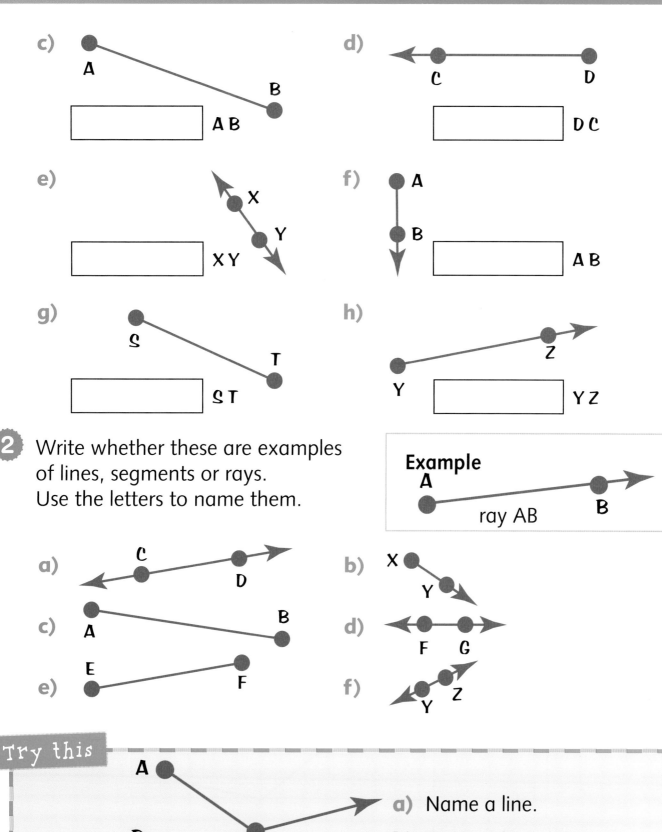

c)

A

B

[ ] A B

d)

C　　　　　D

[ ] D C

e)

X

Y

[ ] X Y

f)

A

B

[ ] A B

g)

S

T

[ ] S T

h)

Z

Y

[ ] Y Z

2 Write whether these are examples of lines, segments or rays. Use the letters to name them.

Example
A

ray AB

B

a) C D

b) X Y

c) A B

d) F G

e) E F

f) Y Z

Try this

A

B

E

D

C

a) Name a line.

b) Name a line segment.

c) Name a ray.

51

Introducing polygons

When line segments join to form a closed shape, they make a polygon.
Polygons are flat shapes with straight sides.

These polygons have 3, 4 and
5 sides.

These polygons all have 4 sides.

This is not a polygon
because it has a curved side.

1 Carefully draw some polygons on squared paper.
Join the ends of each line segment to make the corners of the shapes.

a) 3 different 3-sided shapes

b) 3 different 4-sided shapes

c) 3 different 5-sided shapes

d) 3 different 6-sided shapes

2 Triangles are polygons with 3 sides.

Write **always**, **sometimes** or **never** to complete each sentence.

a) Triangles [   ] have 3 corners.

b) Triangles [   ] have 3 sides the same length.

c) Triangles [   ] have curved sides.

d) Triangles [   ] have 4 corners.

e) Triangles [   ] have 3 sides of different lengths.

f) Triangles [   ] have 3 sides.

3 Draw your own shapes. Join the dots to help. Use a ruler.

a) Draw 3 squares. Make each square different.

b) Draw 3 rectangles. Make each rectangle different.

c) Draw 3 triangles. Make each triangle different.

Squares and rectangles

Look at these shapes.

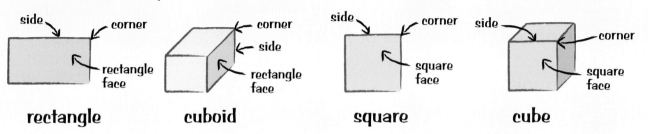

rectangle   cuboid   square   cube

A square is a special rectangle.

- How are the shapes similar to each other?
- How are they different?
- Why is a square a special rectangle?

1 Find the odd shape out in each set. Complete each sentence.

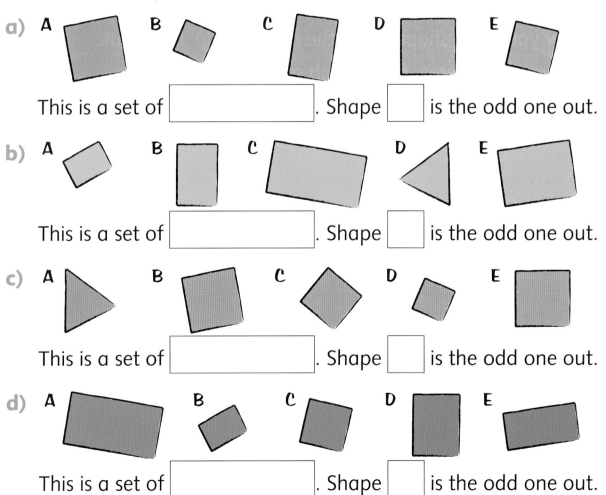

a) A   B   C   D   E

This is a set of [_____]. Shape [ ] is the odd one out.

b) A   B   C   D   E

This is a set of [_____]. Shape [ ] is the odd one out.

c) A   B   C   D   E

This is a set of [_____]. Shape [ ] is the odd one out.

d) A   B   C   D   E

This is a set of [_____]. Shape [ ] is the odd one out.

2 How many rectangles and squares are on each shape?

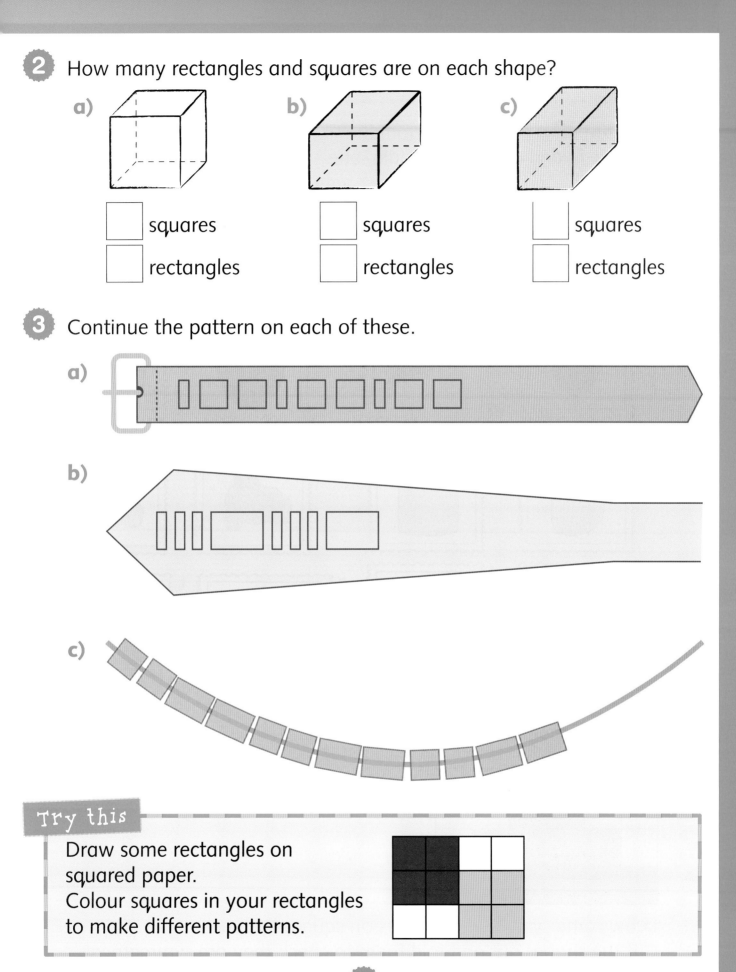

a)

☐ squares

☐ rectangles

b)

☐ squares

☐ rectangles

c)

☐ squares

☐ rectangles

3 Continue the pattern on each of these.

a)

b)

c)

Try this

Draw some rectangles on squared paper.
Colour squares in your rectangles to make different patterns.

Symmetrical shapes

This picture of a butterfly is symmetrical.
When it is folded down the middle, one
half is exactly the same as the other half.

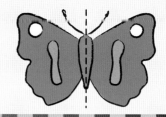

1 Look at these pictures.

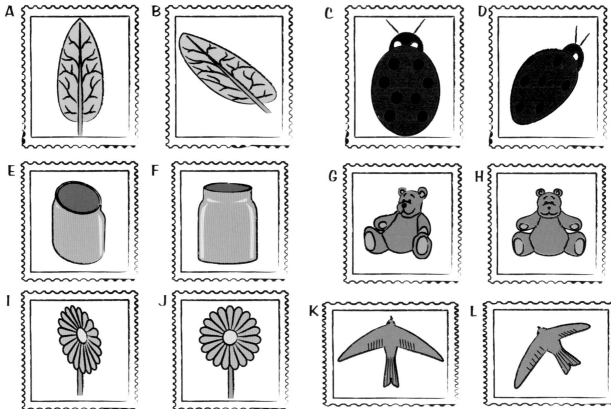

Which of them are symmetrical?
Which of them are not symmetrical?

2 This shape is symmetrical.

Draw some symmetrical shapes on squared paper.
Cut the shapes out and fold them to check they are symmetrical.

3 Draw the reflection of each shape.

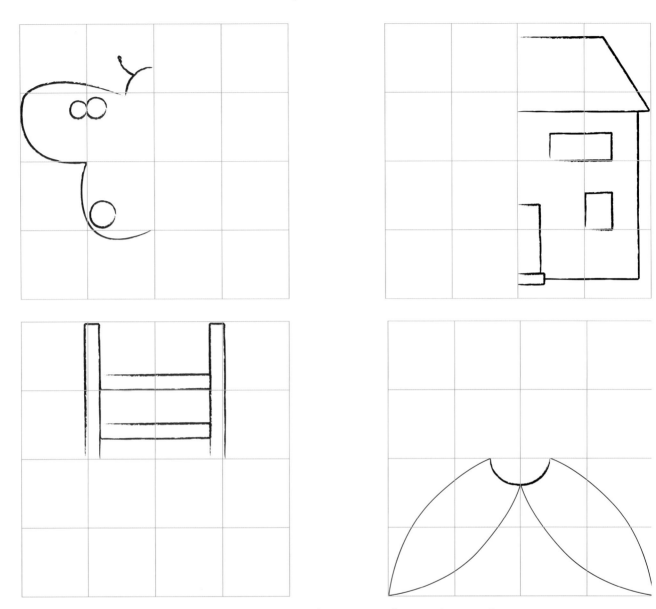

Colour the completed picture. Make sure the coloured pattern is symmetrical.

Put a spot of paint or ink on a piece of paper. Fold it in the middle of the spot and then open it out again. Explore the different symmetrical patterns you can make.

Lines of symmetry

A line of symmetry is like a
mirror line or a fold line.
One half of the shape looks like
the reflection of the other half.

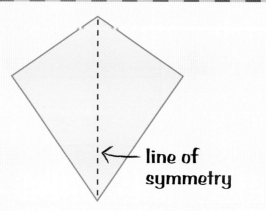

← line of
symmetry

1 Look at these shapes.
Where are the lines of symmetry?
Draw one line of symmetry on each shape.

2 Draw one line of symmetry on each shape.

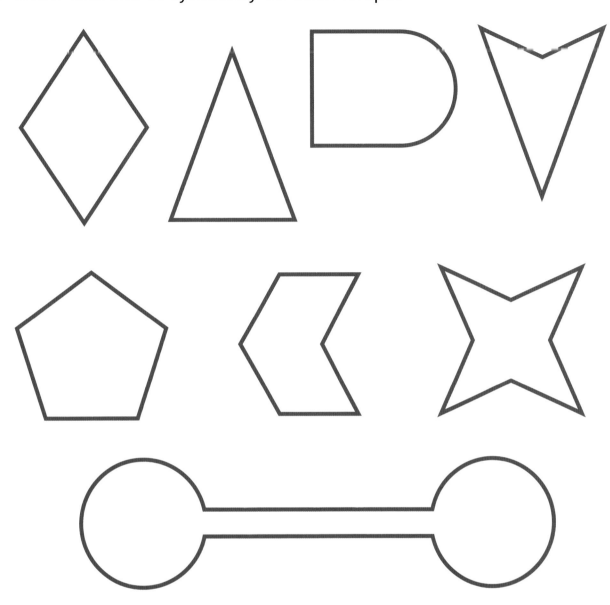

Describe these polygons.

Area: counting squares

The area is the amount of space covered by a shape.

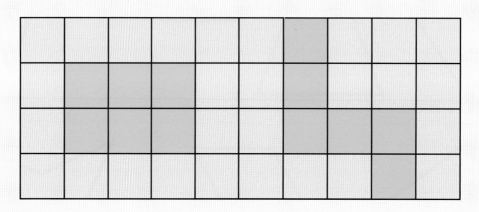

The area of each green shape is 6 squares.

1 Count the squares and write the area of each shape.

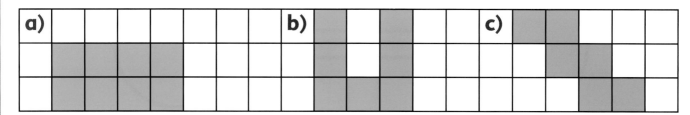

a) Area = ☐ squares   b) Area = ☐ squares   c) Area = ☐ squares

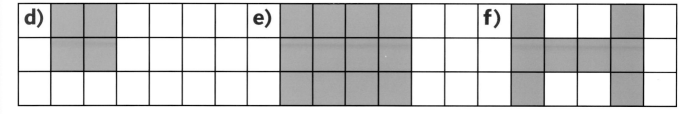

d) Area = ☐ squares   e) Area = ☐ squares   f) Area = ☐ squares

2 Join pairs of shapes with the same area.

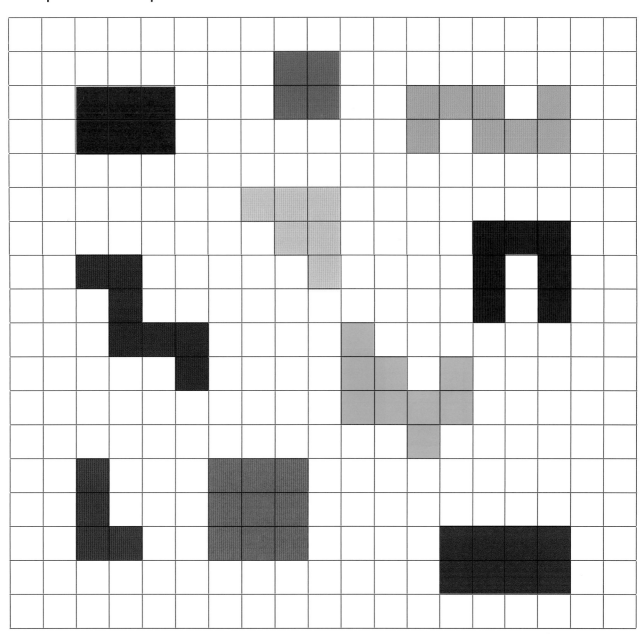

Try this

Use squared paper. Draw different shapes with an area of 6 squares.

How many different shapes can you make?

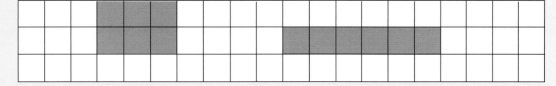

Comparing areas

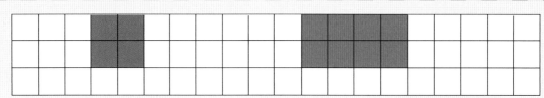

This square has an area of 4 squares.

This rectangle has an area of 8 squares.

Compare the area of each shape.

How much bigger is the rectangle than the square?

1 Find the area of each shape and answer these questions.

a)

How much **bigger** is A than B?

b)

How much **bigger** is A than B?

c)

How much **bigger** is A than B?

d)

How much **smaller** is A than B?

e)

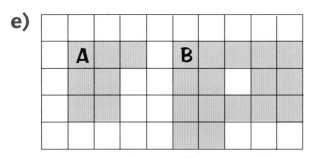

How much **smaller** is A than B?

f)

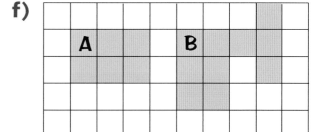

How much **smaller** is A than B?

2 Find the area of each shape and answer these questions.

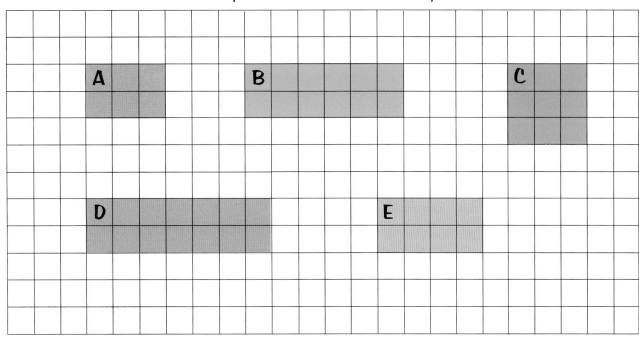

Area of shapes:

A → ☐ squares   B → ☐ squares   C → ☐ squares

D → ☐ squares   E → ☐ squares

a) How much **bigger** is B than C?

b) How much **bigger** is D than A?

c) How much **smaller** is E than C?

d) How much **smaller** is B than D?

Try this

How could you find the area of a curved shape on squared paper?

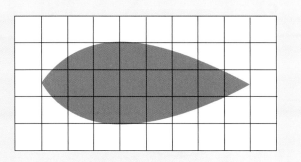

Congruent shapes

If a shape is exactly the same as another shape, the two shapes are **congruent**.

These two rectangles are congruent. They are the same size and the same shape.

How can you check?

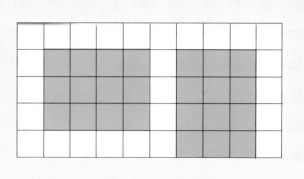

1 Look at the first shape in each row. Which shape is congruent to it?

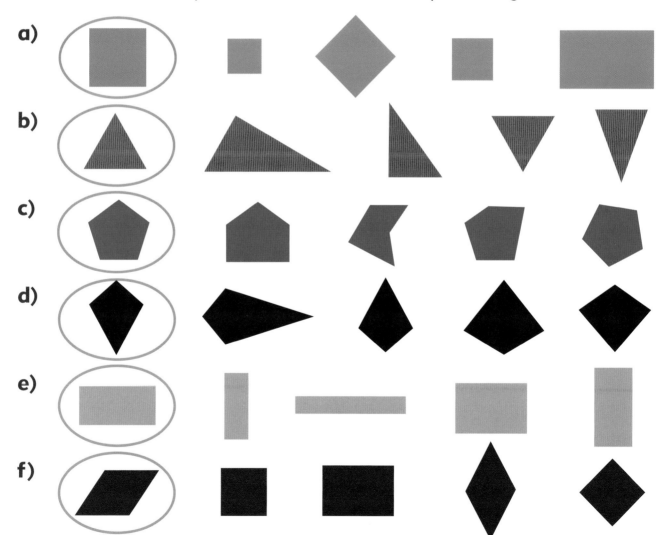

a)

b)

c)

d)

e)

f)

2 Look at the first shape in each row. Which shape is congruent to it?

a)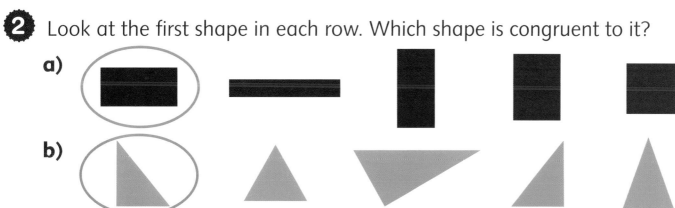

b)

c)

d)

3 This shape is drawn again upside-down.

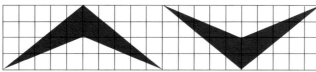

Copy each shape on squared paper and then draw it upside-down.

a)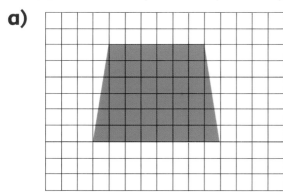

b)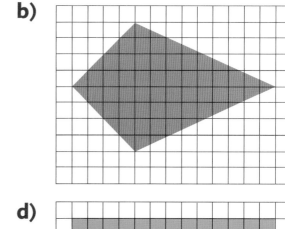

c)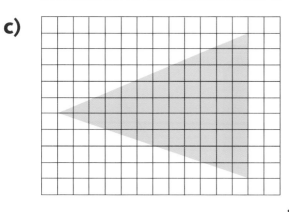

d)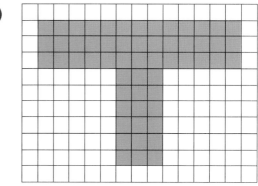

Tiling patterns

This rectangle has an area of 8 squares.

Congruent rectangles like this can be used to make a tiling pattern with no gaps.

1 **a)** Choose a shape to draw and cut out.

b) Cut out six or more congruent shapes.

c) Use them to make your own tiling pattern.

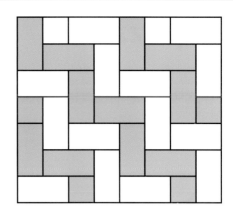

2 Choose one of these shapes as a tile.

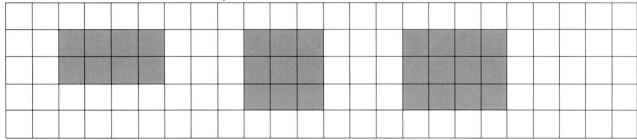

Use it to make a tiling pattern on this grid. Draw and colour your pattern.

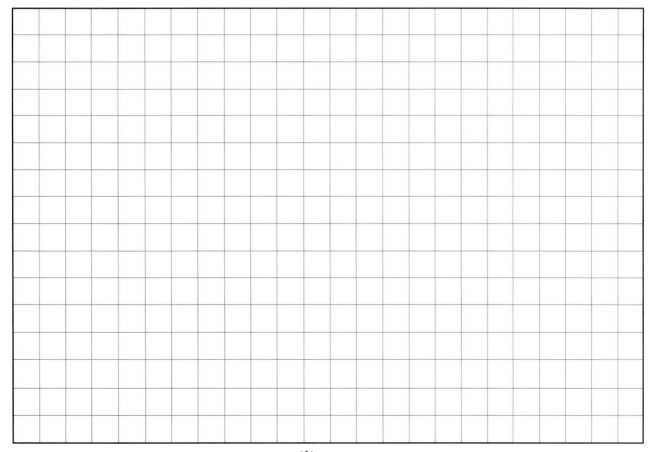

Shape puzzle

Copy this shape puzzle on squared paper.

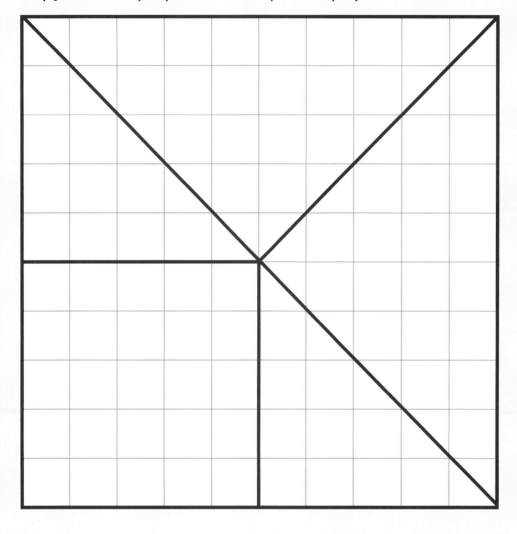

1 Cut out each shape so there are five pieces.
Move them around and put them together to make different shapes.
You can use some or all of the pieces.

a) Put them back together to make the original square.

b) Can you make other squares with the shapes?

c) What is the area of each square?

d) Explore other shapes that you can make with your shape puzzle pieces.

2 Use squared paper to cut out an L-shape.

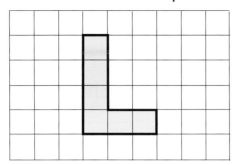

Make 9 or 10 copies of your L-shape.
Use them to make some different tiling patterns.

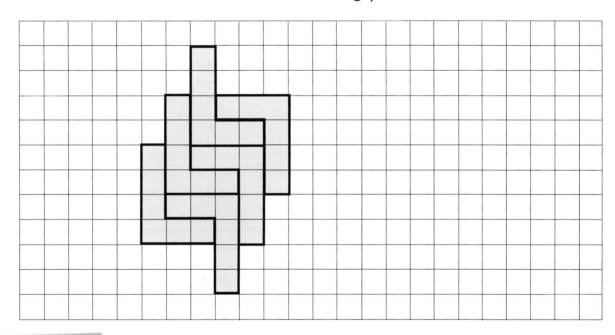

Assessment

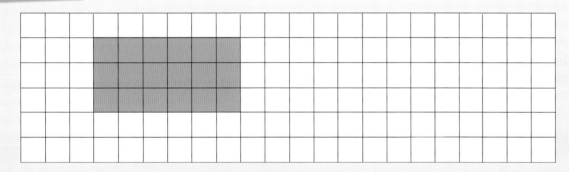

a) What is the name of this shape?

b) What is the area of the shape?

c) What would be the area of a congruent rectangle?

Flat and solid shapes

1 **a)** Complete this chart. Write the shape letters in the correct sections.

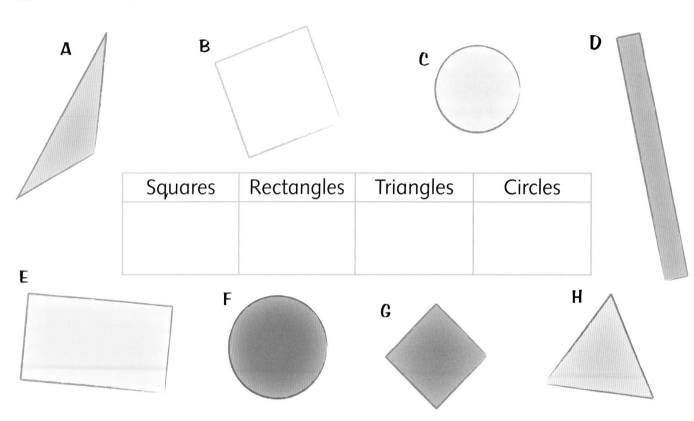

Squares	Rectangles	Triangles	Circles

b) Draw a shape in each box to match the names.
Make each shape different from the ones above.

2 Complete these sentences for each shape.

a)

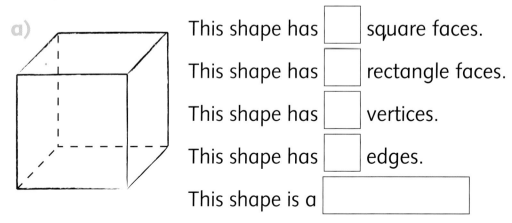

This shape has ☐ square faces.

This shape has ☐ rectangle faces.

This shape has ☐ vertices.

This shape has ☐ edges.

This shape is a ☐

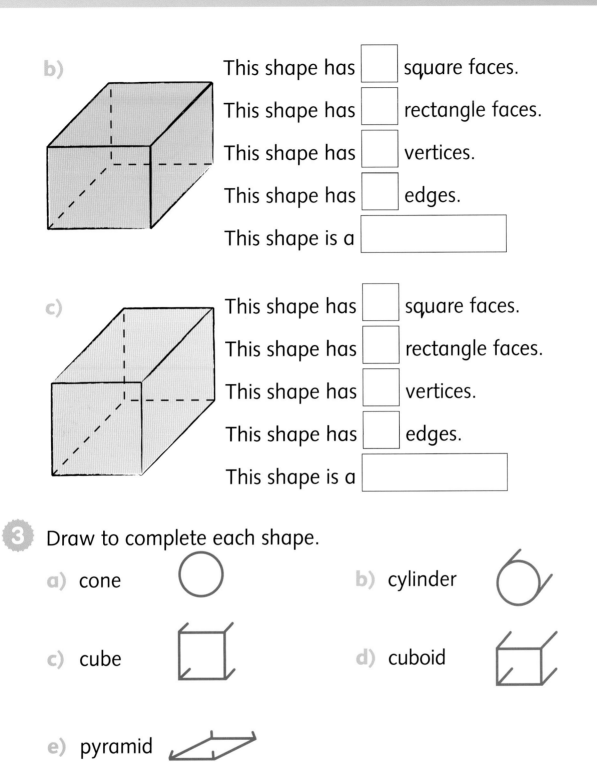

b)

This shape has ☐ square faces.

This shape has ☐ rectangle faces.

This shape has ☐ vertices.

This shape has ☐ edges.

This shape is a ☐

c)

This shape has ☐ square faces.

This shape has ☐ rectangle faces.

This shape has ☐ vertices.

This shape has ☐ edges.

This shape is a ☐

3 Draw to complete each shape.

a) cone

b) cylinder

c) cube

d) cuboid

e) pyramid

Try this

Draw a closed curve and an open curve.
How do they differ?

Lines and shapes

1

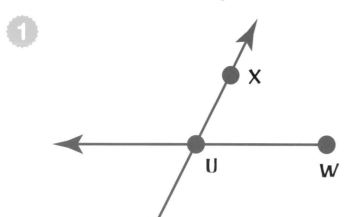
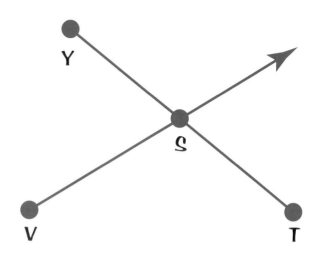

a) Name a line.
b) Name a line segment.
c) Name a ray.

2 Write the name for each shape.
Draw a line of symmetry on each shape.

a)
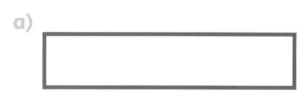

b)
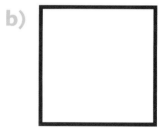

c)
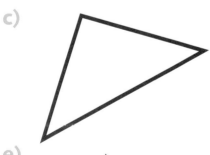

d)
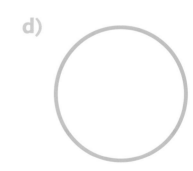

e)

3 Some flat shapes have been sorted on to a diagram.

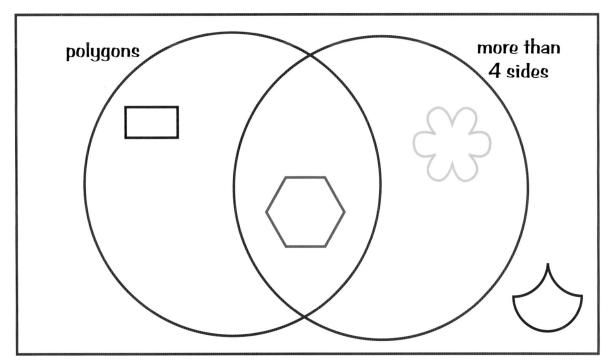

a) Copy the diagram on a large piece of paper.
b) Draw or cut out some shapes and stick them in the correct place on the diagram.

4 Look at the shapes you have put on the sorting diagram.

a) Which shapes are symmetrical?
b) Sort the shapes again so that you have a set of symmetrical shapes and a set that are not symmetrical.

Try this

Complete this pattern so it is symmetrical.

Area of shapes

1 What is the area of each of these shapes?

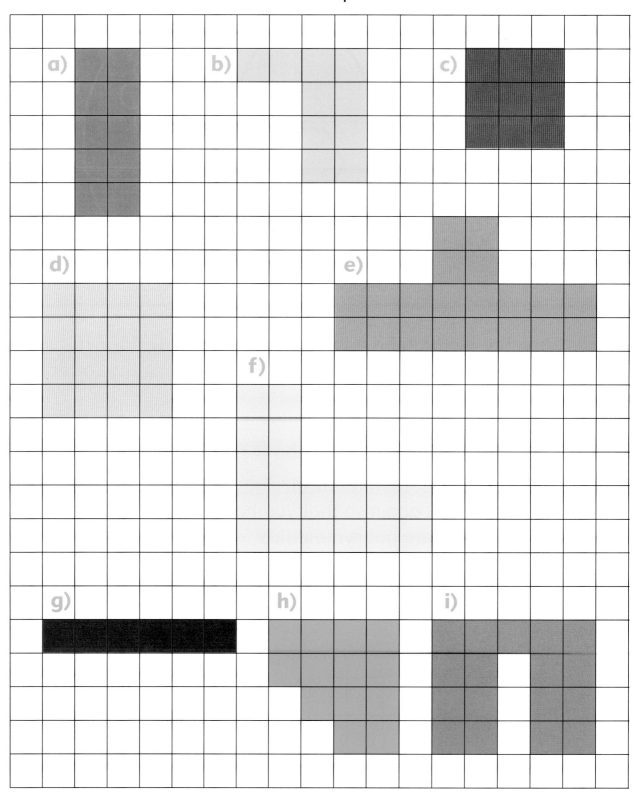

2 Complete these patterns so they are symmetrical.

a)

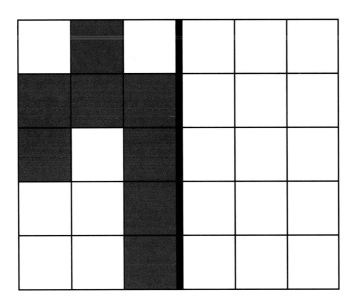

b)

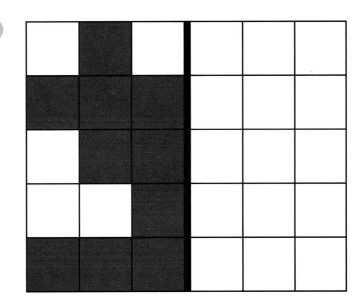

3 What is the area of each of the symmetrical shapes above?

a) area = ☐ squares   b) area = ☐ squares

Draw four different rectangles, each with an area of 24 squares.

Metres

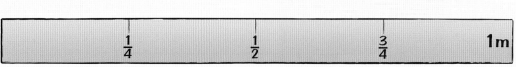

This is a picture of a metre stick.
It is a useful tool for measuring lengths.

1 metre is written as 1 m.

Harry is taller than 1 metre. He is about $1\frac{1}{4}$ m.

1

Look around you at the things in your classroom. Estimate the length of each item in metres. Measure each item with a metre stick.

Copy and complete these sentences for each:

I think the [   ] is about [   ] metres.

The [   ] is about [   ] m.

2 Parts of the body were once used for measuring.
This is about 1 metre on an adult.

Use a metre stick and measure this distance on your friends.
How many people have the same arm length?
Why is it better to use a metre stick than parts of the body like this?

Try this

Measure and mark out a 1 m track on the floor.

a) Try to roll a marble exactly 1 metre.

b) Try to throw a beanbag exactly 1 metre.

c) Turn away from the track. Place two books about 1 metre apart.
Measure the distance. Is it shorter or longer than 1 metre?

Centimetres

A ruler is a useful tool for measuring smaller lengths.
This shows a centimetre ruler.

- Each division is 1 centimetre in length.
- Each small division between the centimetres is $\frac{1}{2}$ centimetre.
- The length of the stick is 6 centimetres, or 6 cm.

1 Look at the ruler above and estimate the length of each of these lines. Use a ruler and measure the exact length. Write your estimate and the exact length.

a) _____

estimate: ☐ cm   length: ☐ cm

b) _____

estimate: ☐ cm   length: ☐ cm

c) _____

estimate: ☐ cm   length: ☐ cm

d) _____

estimate: ☐ cm   length: ☐ cm

e) _____

estimate: ☐ cm   length: ☐ cm

f) _____

estimate: ☐ cm   length: ☐ cm

2 Write the length of each pencil.

a)  [ ] cm

b) [ ] cm

c)  [ ] cm

| 0 | 1 | 2 | 3 | 4 | 5 | 6 | 7 | 8 | 9 | 10 | 11 | 12 | 13 | 14 | 15 |
cm

d)  [ ] cm

e) 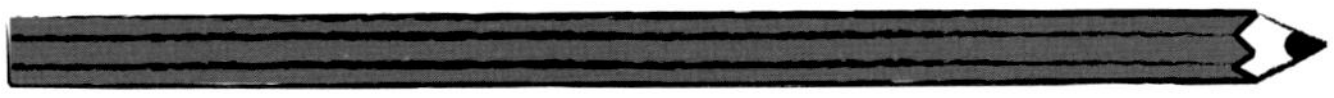 [ ] cm

f)  [ ] cm

Try this

Estimate and measure the lengths of these lines.
Think about how you will measure them.

a)

estimate: [ ] cm   length: [ ] cm

b)

estimate: [ ] cm   length: [ ] cm

Metres and centimetres

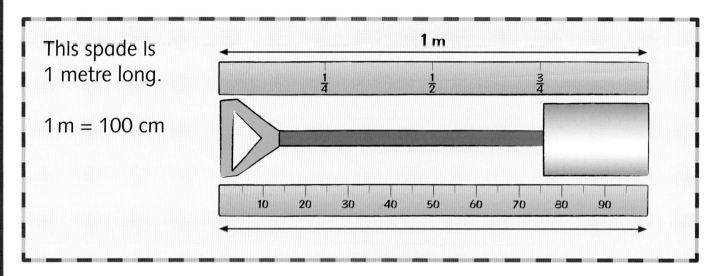

This spade is 1 metre long.

1 m = 100 cm

1 Join the matching pairs.

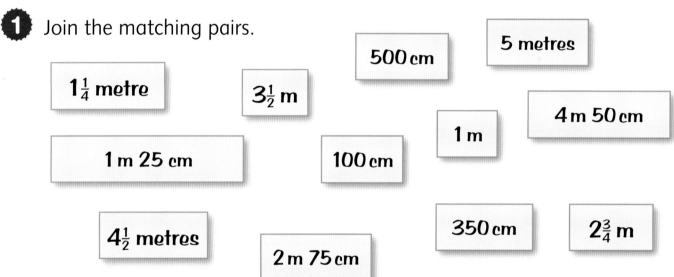

$1\frac{1}{4}$ metre

$3\frac{1}{2}$ m

500 cm

5 metres

4 m 50 cm

1 m 25 cm

100 cm

1 m

$4\frac{1}{2}$ metres

2 m 75 cm

350 cm

$2\frac{3}{4}$ m

2 Find lengths that are the same. Write the matching pairs.
One has been done for you.

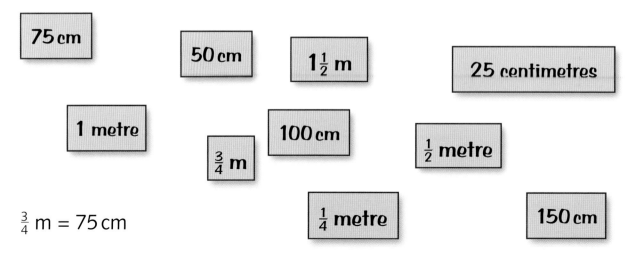

75 cm

50 cm

$1\frac{1}{2}$ m

25 centimetres

1 metre

$\frac{3}{4}$ m

100 cm

$\frac{1}{2}$ metre

$\frac{3}{4}$ m = 75 cm

$\frac{1}{4}$ metre

150 cm

3 Which unit of measurement would you use to measure each item, metres or centimetres?

Example

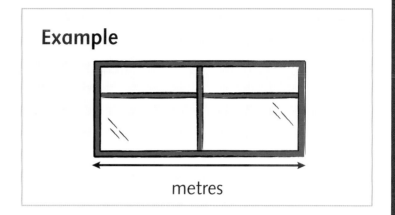

metres

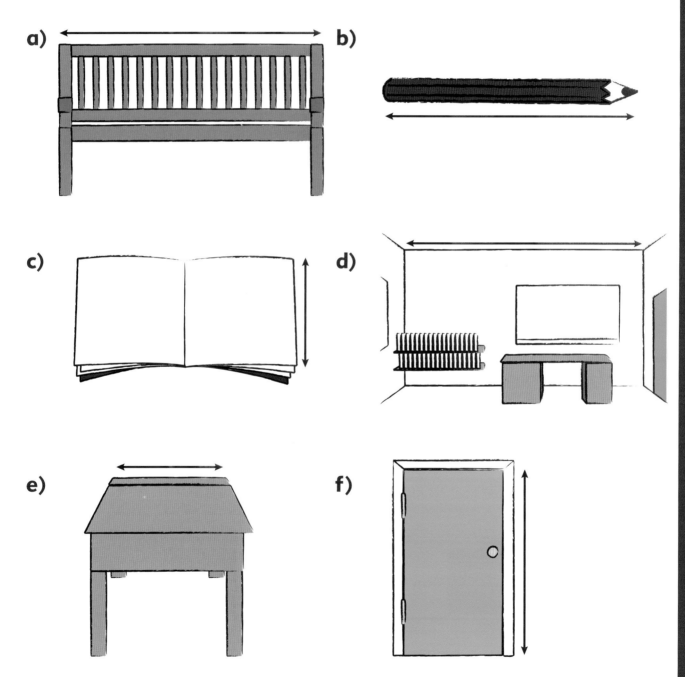

a)

b)

c)

d)

e)

f)

Measuring perimeter

The perimeter of a shape is the distance all around the edge.

5 cm

4 cm   4 cm

5 cm

Add together the length of each side to work out the perimeter of this rectangle.

Perimeter = 5 cm + 4 cm + 5 cm + 4 cm = 18 cm

1 Work out the perimeter of each of these rectangles and squares.

a)
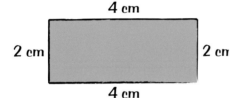
4 cm
2 cm   2 cm
4 cm

Perimeter = ☐ cm

b)
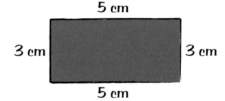
5 cm
3 cm   3 cm
5 cm

Perimeter = ☐ cm

c)
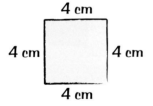
4 cm
4 cm   4 cm
4 cm

Perimeter = ☐ cm

d)
4 cm
3 cm   3 cm
4 cm

Perimeter = ☐ cm

e)
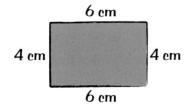
6 cm
4 cm   4 cm
6 cm

Perimeter = ☐ cm

f)
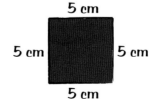
5 cm
5 cm   5 cm
5 cm

Perimeter = ☐ cm

2 Add the lengths of the sides to work out the perimeter of each of these rectangles.

a)

2 cm

4 cm

Perimeter = ☐ cm

b)

3 cm

6 cm

Perimeter = ☐ cm

c)

4 cm

6 cm

Perimeter = ☐ cm

d)

2 cm

5 cm

Perimeter = ☐ cm

e)

4 cm

5 cm

Perimeter = ☐ cm

Try this

Measure these shapes and work out the perimeters.
What do you notice?

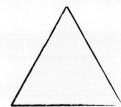
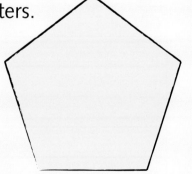

Estimating and measuring lengths

Make a Measuring Mouse like this.
Copy it carefully on to paper and cut it out so it is exactly 10 cm long.

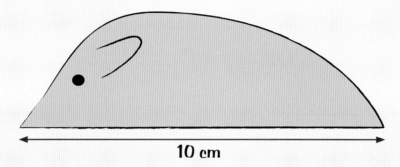

10 cm

Use your Measuring Mouse to measure the length of a pencil.

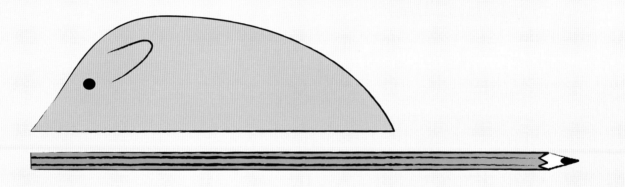

1 Choose five more things to measure.
Complete the chart.

I measured	I estimated	It was
pencil		

2 Estimate the lengths of each of these pieces of thread.
Measure each to see how close your estimate was.

a)

Estimate ➜ ☐ cm   Length ➜ ☐ cm

b)

Estimate ➜ ☐ cm   Length ➜ ☐ cm

c)

Estimate ➜ ☐ cm   Length ➜ ☐ cm

d)

Estimate ➜ ☐ cm   Length ➜ ☐ cm

e)

Estimate ➜ ☐ cm   Length ➜ ☐ cm

Assessment

Cut out some strips of paper of different lengths.
Work with a group to estimate and then measure the length of each
strip to the nearest centimetre.
Record your results and compare your estimates and actual lengths.

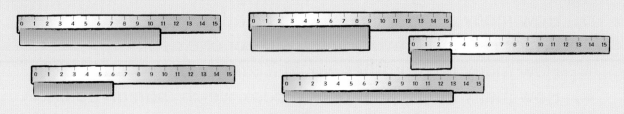

Measuring weight

This book is balanced by 8 cubes.

The book weighs about 8 cubes.

What is the weight of 2 books?

1 book → 8 cubes
2 books → 8 × 2 = 16 cubes

An apple is balanced by 6 cubes.

Which is heavier, the apple or the book?

apple → 6 cubes
book → 8 cubes
The book is heavier.

This paintbrush is balanced by 2 cubes.

How many paintbrushes would weigh about the same as the apple?

1 paintbrush → 2 cubes
1 apple → 6 cubes → 3 paintbrushes

1 Look at the weights of the book, apple and paintbrush.
Answer these.
a) What is the weight, in cubes, of 2 apples?
b) How many cubes will balance 5 paintbrushes?
c) Which is heavier, two paintbrushes or one apple?
d) How many paintbrushes would it take to balance a book?
e) How many more cubes does a book weigh than an apple?
f) What items could balance 10 cubes?

2 Draw the bricks on these balance scales to make each true.

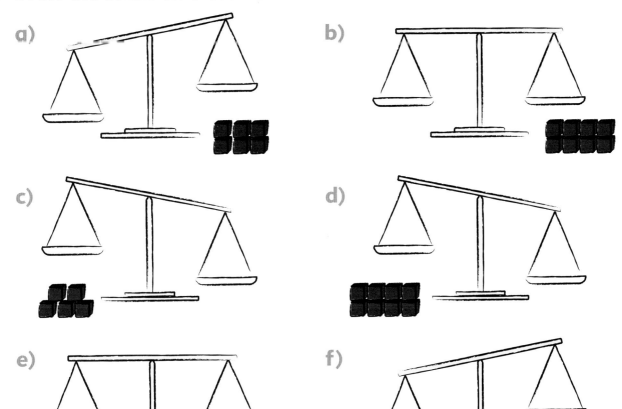

a)

b)

c)

d)

e)

f)

Choose six objects from your classroom. Use marbles, cubes or other items to measure the weight of each object. Record your results.

Object	Number of cubes
pencil	

Kilograms

We use kilograms to measure the weight of objects.

This flour weighs 1 kilogram.
1 kilogram is also written as 1 kg.

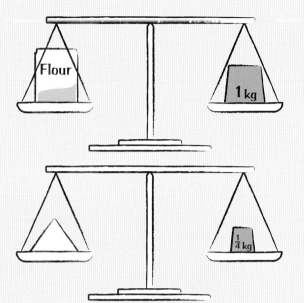

This butter weighs $\frac{1}{2}$ kilogram or $\frac{1}{2}$ kg.   This salt weighs $\frac{1}{4}$ kilogram or $\frac{1}{4}$ kg.

1 Estimate the weight of each object, $\frac{1}{4}$ kg, $\frac{1}{2}$ kg, 1 kg or more than 1 kg.

A
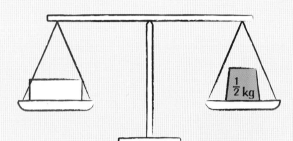

B Tea

C COFFEE

D Washing powder
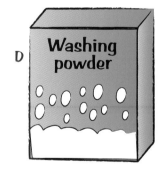

E Rice Family Size

I Cement
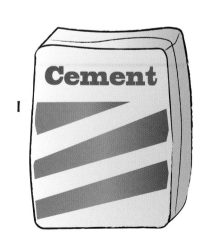

F

G Dates

H Seeds

2 How much does each parcel weigh?

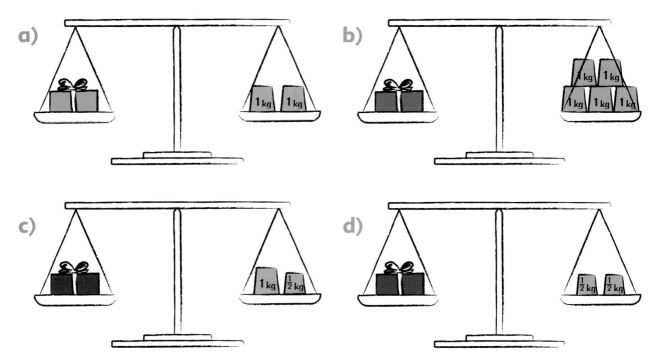

a)

b)

c)

d)

3 Find a selection of objects that you estimate would weigh about 1 kg.
Use balances to check if you are correct.

Record your results.

About the same as 1 kg	Lighter than 1 kg	Heavier than 1 kg

Comparing amounts

We use different containers to measure and compare non countable amounts.

- 6 spoonfuls of water fill the cup.
- 2 cupfuls of water fill the jug.

How many spoonfuls will fill the jug?

2 × 6 = 12 spoonfuls will fill the jug.

1 Each pot fills 3 bowls of soup. Draw the correct number of bowls for each of these.

a)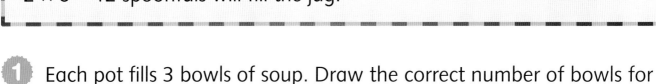

b)

c)

d)

2 Complete each sentence.

a)

4 teaspoons fill 1 tablespoon. 12 teaspoons fill ☐ tablespoons.

b)

3 glasses fill 1 bottle. 9 glasses fill ☐ bottles.

c)

1 teapot fills 5 cups. 4 teapots fill [ ] cups.

d)

1 medicine bottle fills 8 spoons. 2 medicine bottles fill [ ] spoons.

3 Answer these.

a)

2 jugs fill a washing bowl.
4 glasses fill a jug.
How many glasses will fill the bowl?

b)

3 bottles fill a watering can.
10 watering cans fill a barrel.
How many bottles will fill the barrel?

c)

A saucepan fills 4 bowls of soup.
6 spoonfuls fill a bowl.
How many spoonfuls will fill the saucepan?

d)

A kettle fills 3 teapots.
A teapot fills 5 cups.
How many cups will fill the kettle?

Litres

We find out how much liquid there is in a container by finding its capacity.
The litre is a standard unit for measuring capacity.

This bowl holds 3 litres or 3 l of water.

1 Use a litre jug and some different containers.

Use the litre measure to work out which holds more and which hold less than 1 litre of water.
Complete the chart.

About the same as 1 litre	Less than 1 litre	More than 1 litre

2 Use the containers that are less than 1 litre from question 1.
Estimate how many of each container are needed to fill the 1 litre jug.

3 Draw a line from each container to the correct capacity in each jug.

Less than 1 litre   About 1 litre   More than 1 litre

Try this

This chart shows the capacity of different containers.

Container	Number of each needed to fill a bucket
bottle	5
cup	8
jug	4
glass	10
pot	2

Use the information to answer these questions.
a) Which is the smallest container?
b) Which is the largest container?
c) How many glasses of water would fill a bottle?
d) How many cups of water would fill a jug?
e) How many glasses of water would fill a pot?

Measures problems

When you read a problem, try to 'picture' the problem.
Try these four steps.
1 Read the problem.
2 Sort out the calculation.
3 Work out the answer.
4 Check back.

Elizabeth has 3 kg of flour. She uses $1\frac{1}{2}$ kg to make some bread.
How much flour does she have left?

$3\,kg - 1\frac{1}{2}\,kg = 1\frac{1}{2}\,kg$ of flour left.
Check: $1\frac{1}{2}\,kg + 1\frac{1}{2}\,kg = 3\,kg$

1 Read and answer these.

a) What is the difference in height between two baobob trees measuring 24 m and 15 m?

b)  At Market Rosie had a pot with 32 litres of soup. After an hour she had 14 litres left. How many litres had she sold?

c) Two parcels weigh a total of $3\frac{1}{2}$ kg. One of the parcels weighs 2 kg. How much does the other parcel weigh?

d)  A lemon drink is made with $\frac{1}{2}$ litre of lemonade and 6 litres of water. How much lemon drink is there in total?

e)  A farmer picks two bunches of palm oil fruit weighing $1\frac{1}{2}$ kg and $2\frac{1}{2}$ kg. How much do they weigh together?

f) Charlie drives 18 km to see his Grandfather on Friday. On Saturday he drives 23 km back home, stopping off at his Aunt's on the way. How far did he travel in total over the two days?

1 Colour the correct amount of water in each jug.

a) 1 litre

b) $\frac{1}{4}$ litre

c) $\frac{1}{2}$ litre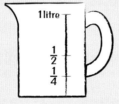

d) 2 litres

e) $\frac{1}{2}$ litre

f) $3\frac{1}{2}$ litres

2 You need a jug or bottle.

a) Estimate its capacity. Measure to check.

b) Estimate its weight when full of water. Measure to check.

c) Estimate its height. Measure to check.

Unit 23 Handling data

Using tallies

You can use tally marks when you count objects.

| || ||| |||| |||| |||| | |||| || |||| ||| |||| ||| |||| |||| |
1 2 3 4 5 6 7 8 9 10 11

|||| |||| || |||| |||| ||| |||| |||| |||| |||| |||| |||| |||| |||| |||| |
12   13   14   15   16

|||| |||| |||| || |||| |||| |||| ||| |||| |||| |||| |||| |||| |||| |||| ||||
17   18   19   20

1 Write numbers to match these tally marks.

a) |||| ||||
   |||| |||| ||

b) |||| |||| ||||
   |||| ||||

c) |||| |||| |||
   |||| ||||

d) |||| |||| ||||
   |||| |||| ||||

e) |||| |||| ||||
   |||| |||| ||||

f) |||| |||| |||| ||||
   |||| |||| |||| |

g) |||| |||| |||| ||||
   |||| |||| ||||

h) |||| |||| |||| ||||
   |||| |||| |

i) |||| |||| |||| ||||
   |||| |||| |||| |||| |

j) |||| |||| |||| ||||
   |||| |||| |||| |||| |||

2 Draw tally marks for each of these.

a) 26 b) 21 c) 32 d) 27 e) 35
f) 24 g) 28 h) 33 i) 39 j) 40

3 This tally chart shows how many of each type of drink was sold from a stall in one day. Write the totals for each drink.

Drink	Tallies	Total
tea	|||| ||||	
coffee	|||| |||| ||||	
lemonade	||||	
orange juice	|||| |||| ||||		
bottled water	|||| |||	

a) How many more teas were sold than bottled water?
b) Which drink was bought 16 times?
c) How many teas and coffees were sold altogether?
d) How many fewer lemonades than orange juices were sold?
e) How many drinks were sold altogether?

4 A school carried out a survey of birthdays.
This chart shows how many birthdays fell on each day of the week.

Day	Tally	Total
Sunday	卌 卌 卌 II	
Monday	卌 卌 卌 卌 卌	
Tuesday	卌 卌 卌 卌 卌 II	
Wednesday	卌 卌 卌 卌 II	
Thursday	卌 卌 卌 IIII	
Friday	卌 卌 卌 卌	
Saturday	卌 卌 卌 I	

a) Write the totals for each day.
b) On which day were there 25 birthdays?
c) How many birthdays were on a Saturday?
d) How many more birthdays were on a Tuesday than on a Thursday?
e) On which day was there two fewer birthdays than on a Wednesday?

Carry out your own birthday survey.
Record your results on a tally chart.

Counting columns

Here are some toy animals.

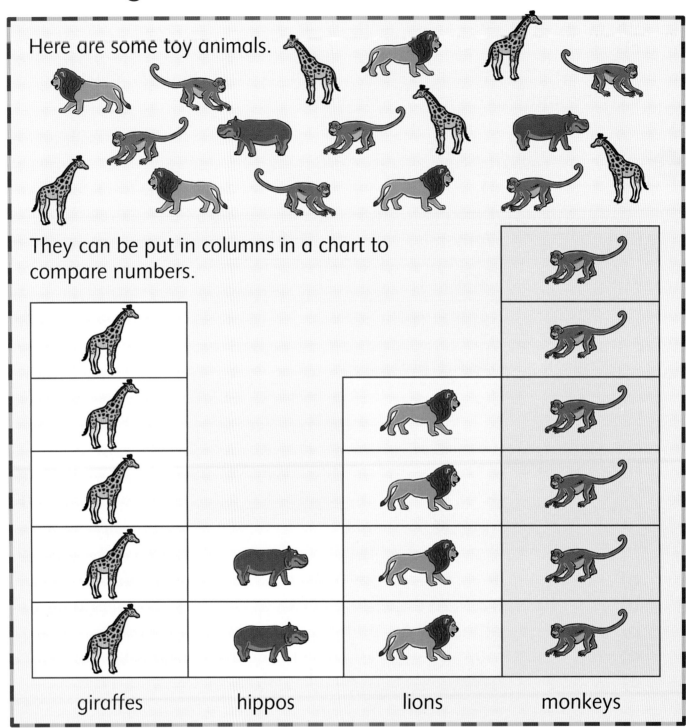

They can be put in columns in a chart to compare numbers.

giraffes   hippos   lions   monkeys

1 a) How many giraffes are there?
   b) How many more monkeys are there than hippos?
   c) How many more monkeys than lions?
   d) How many fewer hippos than giraffes?
   e) How many toy animals are there altogether?

2 This chart shows the numbers of different coloured sweets in a bag.

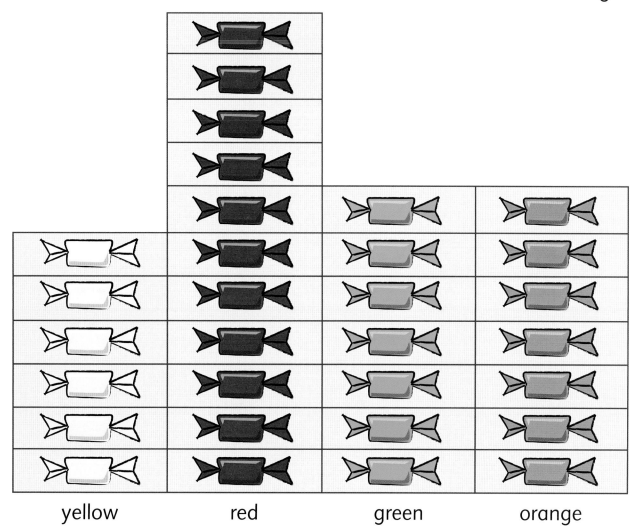

yellow   red   green   orange

a) How many orange sweets are there?
b) Which two sweet colours had the same number?
c) How many more red sweets are there than green sweets?
d) How many yellow and green sweets are there altogether?
e) How many sweets were in the bag altogether?

Try this

Carry out a survey of the favourite fruit in
your class.
Choose five different fruits and ask each
child to choose one as their favourite.
Record the results in a chart with pictures of the fruit.

Pictograms

Robert	⚽ ⚽ ⚽ ⚽
Anna	⚽ ⚽ ⚽ ⚽ ⚽ ⚽ ⚽
Katie	⚽ ⚽ ⚽ ⚽ ⚽
Michael	⚽ ⚽ ⚽ ⚽ ⚽ ⚽ ⚽ ⚽ ⚽
Daisy	⚽ ⚽ ⚽

Key: ⚽ = 1 catch

1 Use the pictogram above to answer these.
   a) Who made the most catches?
   b) Who made two more catches than Daisy?
   c) How many catches did Anna make?
   d) How many balls were not caught by Robert?

2 This pictogram shows the different types of pizzas sold in a day.

Type of pizza	
Cheese	🍕 🍕 🍕 🍕 🍕 🍕 🍕 🍕
Seafood	🍕 🍕 🍕 🍕 🍕 🍕 🍕
Margherita	🍕 🍕 🍕
Chicken and pineapple	🍕 🍕 🍕 🍕 🍕 🍕

Key: 🍕 = 2 pizzas

Use the pictogram to answer these.

a) Which type of pizza sold most?
b) For which type of pizza were 12 sold?
c) How many Seafood pizzas were sold?
d) How many Margherita pizzas were sold?
e) How many more Cheese pizzas were sold than Seafood pizzas?
f) How many Seafood and Margherita pizzas were sold altogether?

3 Carry out an experiment to compare colours picked out of a bag.
a) Cut out 10 small pieces of paper all the same size.
b) Colour 4 of them red, 3 blue, 2 green and 1 yellow.

c) Shake them up in a bag or box and pick one out without looking at it.

d) Record the colour in a tally chart and then put it back in the bag.

Colour	Tally
red	
blue	
green	
yellow	

e) Repeat this 20 times (or more).

f) Draw a pictogram to show your results.

Colour	Number of times picked out
red	
blue	
green	
yellow	

g) Describe your results to someone else.

Bar charts

Bar charts show information as bars.

This bar chart shows the number of books that were read by some children in a term at school.

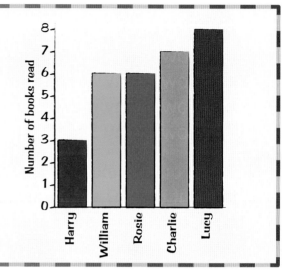

1
a) Who read 7 books?
b) How many books did Harry read?
c) How many more books did Lucy read than William?
d) How many children read more than 5 books?
e) How many books were read by this group altogether?

2 This graph shows the flavours of ice creams sold from a store in a day.

a) Which was the most popular flavour?
b) How many mint chip flavour ice creams were sold?
c) Which flavour was sold 8 times?
d) How many more chocolate ice creams were sold than coconut ice creams?
e) Which two ice cream flavours sold the same number?

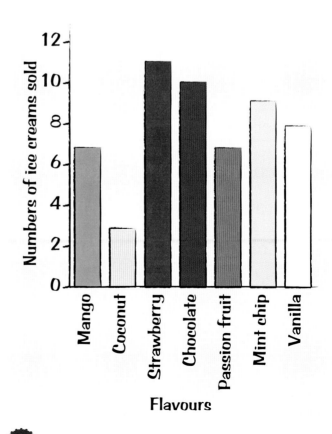

3 A group of children were asked about their favourite activities.
This bar chart shows the results.

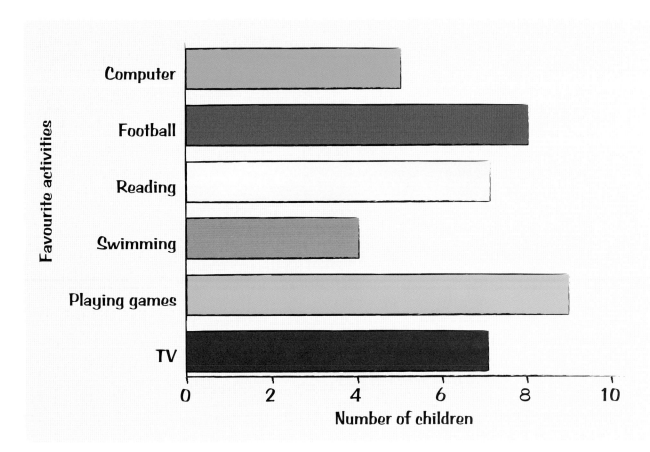

a) Which activity was chosen the most?

b) How many children chose swimming?

c) Which activities were chosen by more than 6 children?

d) Which activity did 5 children choose?

e) What was the total for using a computer and watching TV?

Try this

Carry out your own survey of favourite activities in your class.
Record your results as a bar chart.

Measuring and data

These strips of paper were cut to go around these four bottles.
They were then put in order of length.

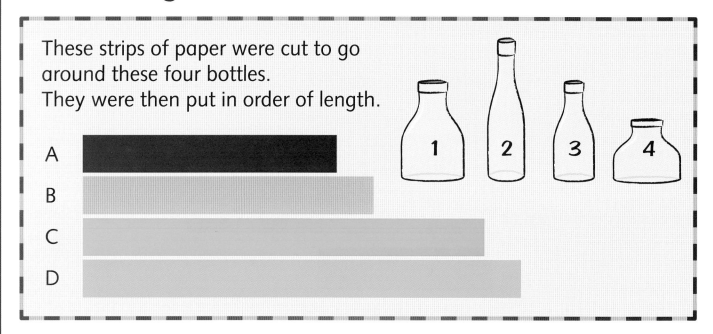

A

B

C

D

1 **a)** Match each bottle to the paper strips.

b) Do you think the bottle with the longest strip will hold the most water?

c) Do you think the height of the bottle is important?

2 Measure the length of each strip. Draw bars to show them on this graph.

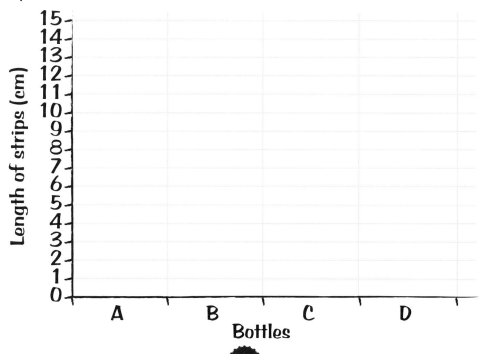

3 Carry out your own experiment with bottles.

   a) You need a selection of different bottles and containers.
   b) Cut strips of paper that fit around each bottle.
   c) Arrange them in order on a graph.
   d) Fill the bottles and compare them.

Do the longer strips match the bottles that hold the most water?

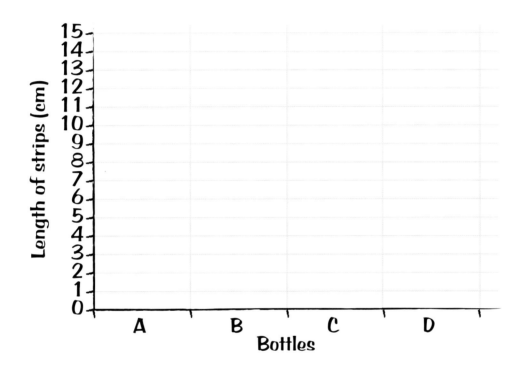

Carry out an experiment with five friends to test your catching skills. Take turns to catch a ball 20 times.

Keep a tally of your score and draw a tally chart.

Draw a graph or pictogram to show your results.

Measuring length

1 Match these lengths to the correct label.
Use a metre stick to check.

about 1 metre	about 2 metres	less than 1 metre

more than 2 metres	between 1 metre and 2 metres

height of chair

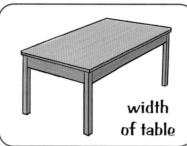

width of table

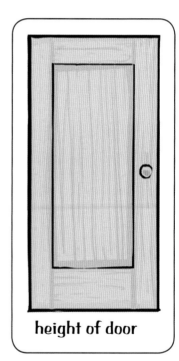

height of door

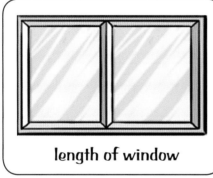

length of window

your height

width of room

length of stride

2   A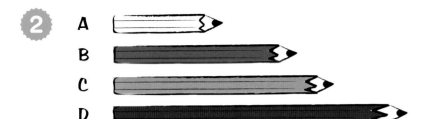
   B
   C
   D

Estimate the lengths of these, then measure them with a ruler.

3   Draw a line from each spot to exactly the length given.

   a) 10 cm   •

   b) 6 cm   •

   c) 13 cm   •

   d) 2 cm   •

4   What is the perimeter of this piece of paper?

5 cm
4 cm   Perimeter = ☐ cm

5   Which of these shapes has the largest perimeter?

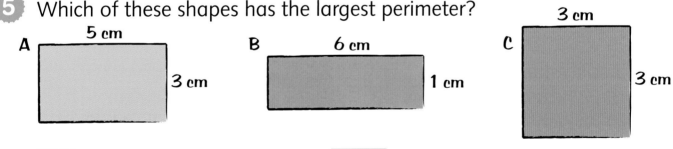

A   5 cm
    3 cm

B   6 cm
    1 cm

C   3 cm
    3 cm

☐ has the largest perimeter of ☐ cm.

Try this

Draw four different rectangles.
Each of them must have a perimeter of 20 cm.

Measures problems

1 Look at these objects and complete the chart

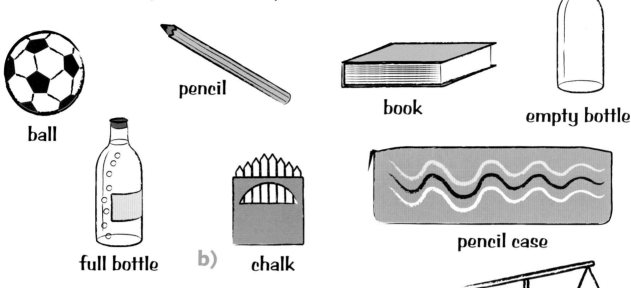

ball

pencil

book

empty bottle

full bottle

b) chalk

pencil case

Use some balance scales and test each object.
Record your results.

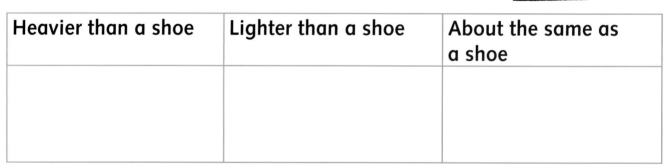

Heavier than a shoe	Lighter than a shoe	About the same as a shoe

2 Balance the objects above with a 1 kg weight.
  a) Which objects weigh more than 1 kg?
  b) Which items can you put together to weigh exactly 1 kg?

3 **a)** Write how many you **think** it will take to fill the jug with these containers.

1 litre

b) Now fill a jug with water using each container. Write how many it took to fill the jug.

Container	Estimate	Check
(cup)	☐ cups	☐ cups
(spoon)	☐ spoons	☐ spoons
(bottle)	☐ bottles	☐ bottle
(jar)	☐ jars	☐ jars

Choose two of your own containers to complete the table.

4 Estimate how many cups can be filled from a litre jug.

Check by pouring. Use tallies to record.
Try this with other containers.

1 litre

I used	My estimate	My measure
cup		
spoon		
bottle		

Handling data

This pictogram shows the number of cars passing school between 10.00 am and 3.00 pm.

Key: = 1 car

1 Use the pictogram to answer these.
   a) How many cars passed school between 10.00 and 11.00?
   b) How many cars passed school between 12.00 and 1.00?
   c) How many more cars passed school between 1.00 and 2.00 than between 2.00 and 3.00?
   d) At which time did 5 cars go by?
   e) At which time did 15 cars go by?

2 Measure the lengths of the hand-spans of you and some friends.

Measure the lengths to the nearest centimetre. Record the results in this bar chart.

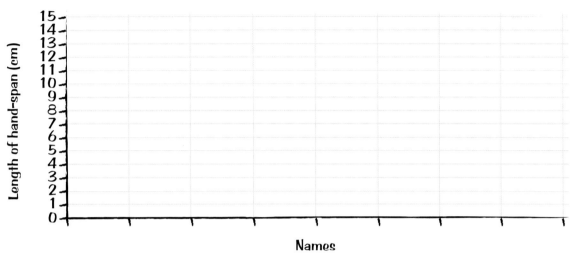

Names

3 These are the distances a group of children can throw a ball.
Look at the bar chart and answer these questions.

a) Who threw the ball 11 metres?

b) How far did Diana throw the ball?

c) How much further did Max throw the ball than Emma?

d) What is the difference between the length of the throws of Tom and Sam?

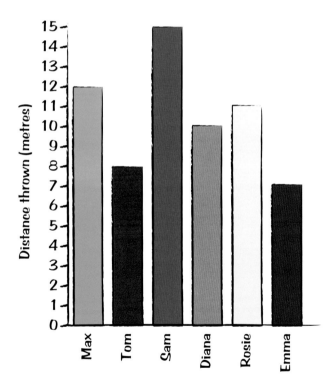

Try this

Measure the distances you and a group of friends can throw a ball. Measure the distances to the nearest metre. Record the results in a bar chart.

Macmillan Education
4 Crinan Street
London N1 9XW
A division of Macmillan Publishers Limited
Companies and representatives throughout the world.

ISBN 978-0-230-02819-7

Designed by Andy Magee Design
Typeset by Tek-Art, Crawley Down, West Sussex
Illustrated by Tek-Art
Cover design by Bigtop Design Limited
The Authors and publishers wish to thank the following for permission to reproduce their photographs:
Cover Photography: Clark Wiseman/www.studio-8.co.uk

Printed and bound in Malaysia

2017   2016   2015   2014
12   11   10 9   8   7